CW01158030

The R. M. Jones Lectures in the Development of Ideas

LEGAL EVOLUTION

LEGAL EVOLUTION
The story of an idea

PETER STEIN
*Regius Professor of Civil Law in the
University of Cambridge and
Fellow of Queens' College*

CAMBRIDGE UNIVERSITY PRESS
CAMBRIDGE
LONDON   NEW YORK   NEW ROCHELLE
MELBOURNE   SYDNEY

Published by the Press Syndicate of the University of Cambridge
The Pitt Building, Trumpington Street, Cambridge CB2 1RP
32 East 57th Street, New York, NY 10022, USA
296 Beaconsfield Parade, Middle Park, Melbourne 3206, Australia

© Cambridge University Press 1980

First published 1980

Printed in Great Britain
at the University Press, Cambridge

Library of Congress Cataloguing in Publication Data
Stein, Peter, 1926–
Legal evolution.
Includes index.
1. Law – History and criticism. 2. Sociological jurisprudence. 3. Law – Philosophy. 4. Natural law.
I. Title.
K150.S74   340'.09   78-73963
ISBN 0 521 22783 6

TO
ANNE

Contents

	Preface	ix
1	The natural law tradition	1
2	Scottish philosophical history of law	23
3	The German historical school of law	51
4	The heyday of legal evolution	69
5	The aftermath of *Ancient Law*	99
	Conclusion	122
	Index	129

Preface

Theories of social evolution have attracted much recent attention but theories of legal evolution have been less intensively investigated. Social evolution and legal evolution are related to each other, and to some extent shared the same fate, but legal evolution has a history of its own, which begins in the eighteenth century.

Eighteenth-century legal theory was closely associated with moral philosophy. Both had grown out of a natural law tradition that used man's rational and social nature everywhere as the basis on which it founded both his moral and his legal obligations to his fellow men in all societies. As the century progressed, however, there was a growing consciousness of differences in this area, differences between a man's moral duties and his legal duties, between his legal duties in different countries and between his legal duties in the same country in different periods.

There were good reasons for this consciousness of differences to be stronger in Britain than elsewhere. English legal thinkers (although not all English lawyers) had long been exercised to account for the distinctive character of the English common law in comparison both with the civil law of continental Europe and with the Scots law in force in the northern part of the recently united kingdom. They had tended to explain the differences as being, in a general way, due to the peculiar features of the English national character. Already in 1704, Thomas Wood, introducing a book on Roman law, assured his English readers that 'the Laws of this Nation (as they are now mixed and tempered) suit admirably to the genius of our people'.[1] Scottish legal thinkers were even more aware of legal differences than their southern brethren, for

---

[1] *A New Institute of the Imperial or Civil Law* (London, 1704), vi.

it was the distinctive Scots law, together with the Kirk, which preserved the separate identity of the Scottish nation after the Union, and it was a matter of debate whether the retention of two systems of law in the one kingdom was justified.

It was in this climate of opinion that the need arose for a theory that explained legal change. Prevailing views of law were not very helpful. Some thought of law as immemorial custom, the heritage of a particular people; others thought of it as the expression of the sovereign's will; and others again regarded it as the product of reason. But none of these conceptions of law provided a satisfactory explanation of how law changes. Was it the restoration of the good, old law, which had somehow become corrupted; was it that the sovereign had changed his mind; or was it that reason had produced rules, which had turned out to be unreasonable? Certain Scottish thinkers suggested that law changes in accordance with changes in society, and that just as society progresses according to certain stages, so the rights and duties prescribed by the law develop in a corresponding way. So legal differences could be accounted for by the fact that the societies in question had reached different stages of development.

In the nineteenth century, the ideas of these Scottish writers were largely forgotten or ignored. Sir Frederick Pollock could seriously assert that before the publication of Maine's *Ancient Law*, 'it was an unheard of process to show that [similarities and anomalies] were really natural products in the development of legal conceptions'.[2] Nineteenth-century legal thinkers, seeking a theory that explained legal change otherwise than simply as the enactment of reform by a legislature, tried to be scientific, and a scientific inquiry was an historical inquiry. It was the German historical school which popularised the notion that a nation's law developed as the nation itself developed, and the idea was taken up with enthusiasm in Britain. It was assumed that legal institutions had a natural history of their own. Evolution and the historical method became synonymous. Pollock again proclaimed, 'The doctrine of evolution is nothing else than the historical method applied to the facts of nature; the historical method is nothing else than the doctrine of evolution applied to known societies and institutions.'[3]

[2] *Oxford Lectures* (London, 1890), 158.   [3] *Oxford Lectures*, 41.

PREFACE

As one of the editors of Adam Smith's *Lectures on Jurisprudence*, I became interested in his ideas on the nature of legal change, and as a student of Roman law, I was struck by the special role of Roman law in the subsequent development of those ideas. The invitation to deliver the R. M. Jones Lectures at Queen's University Belfast, in April 1978, seemed to offer an opportunity to look further into the history of the idea of legal evolution. The leading ideas of some of the main figures in the story are familiar to all students of jurisprudence, but it seemed worthwhile to try to relate those ideas to each other in the context of the legal thought of their times.

I wish to express my sincere thanks to the Vice-Chancellor of Queen's University, Dr Peter Froggatt, for his personal interest in the lectures, and for the generous hospitality which I enjoyed with him and his family in Belfast; to my friends in the Law Faculty at Queen's, and especially its Dean, Colin Campbell, and to the 'discussants' of the lectures, John Burrow, Alan Harding and Paul O'Higgins, from all of whom I learned much; and to my daughter Barbara for help with the Index.

PETER STEIN

I

The natural law tradition

In the early eighteenth century, the usual explanation of the origin of the state, or 'civil society', as it was called, began by postulating an original state of nature, in which primitive man lived on his own. He had few social relationships with other men, and was subject to neither government nor law. This state of nature was converted into civil society by means of a 'social contract'. A group of individuals came together and agreed to live as a community instead of in isolation. The main feature of this explanation was its emphasis on the notion that society was based on the consent of the original members, and this in turn made it possible to argue that ultimately all governments derive their authority from the consent of their subjects. The medieval view had been that governments derive their authority from God, and that the king was God's delegate, who must be obeyed precisely for that reason. The theory of the social contract was thus a rejection of the notion that the power and authority of the king and his government are God-given. In an age when religious freedom was being asserted, it was important to separate man's civil and political duties from his religious obligations.

Social contract theorists did not agree about the character of the state of nature and put forward various versions of the social contract itself. Was the state of nature an actual historical condition through which mankind had passed, or was it rather an intellectual idea, designed to explain in a vivid way the need for men to live in a society under a government? Was it, as Thomas Hobbes thought, a nasty jungle from which man would want to escape at all costs, or was it, as John Locke believed, a more pleasant place, which man would be prepared to leave only on certain conditions which were clearly likely to be to his advantage?

In answer to the suggestion that there seemed to be little evidence of an actual original state of nature, John Locke was quite unabashed, and argued that we must assume its existence:

> It is not at all to be wonder'd, that History gives us but very little account of Men, that lived together in the State of Nature...if we may not suppose Men ever to have been in a State of Nature, because we hear not much of them in such a state, we may as well suppose the armies of Salmanasser, or Xerxes, were never Children, because we hear little of them, till they were Men, and imbodied in Armies. Government is everywhere antecedent to Records...For 'tis with Commonwealths as with particular Persons, they are commonly ignorant of their own Births and Infancies (*Of Civil Government*, sec. 101).

The nature of the contract to form a society would manifestly depend on the kind of state of nature in which the contracting parties lived. In practice it also depended on the political aims of its protagonists. Thomas Hobbes, who was a supporter of the Crown in its struggle with Parliament, argued that the state of nature must have been so dangerous and unpleasant for man that he would gladly agree to surrender all the freedom and power over himself, which he had hitherto enjoyed, to a sovereign person or body who was strong enough to protect him from its perils. Having made such a contract of submission, man would be bound, with only slight reservations, to treat whatever the sovereign commanded as law and therefore to obey it. The law of such a society thus consisted of the commands of whoever was sovereign in that society. If law is the product of the human will, the process of legal change is simple. The sovereign decides to issue a new rule to replace the old rule; he has changed his mind. Of course, a wise sovereign will not issue capricious or arbitrary orders to his subjects. He will try to follow the dictates of common sense, to behave rationally and to issue orders appropriate to his subjects' condition. But whether he succeeds or not does not affect the validity of his commands. They are law because they emanate from him.

John Locke, on the other hand, supported those who made the Glorious Revolution of 1688, which replaced one king with another. He argued that civil society was consciously created by rational men in a state of nature, who first agreed to combine in a community by one contract, and then, by another and separate contract, agreed to entrust its government to a ruler chosen by themselves.

According to this view, the ruler was limited in what he could command his subjects to do, and these limitations were prescribed by nature. Nature endowed men with certain inalienable rights, among them life and property, which they could not surrender.

Although social contract theorists rejected the king as God's intermediary with man, people were still anxious to know what was God's will for man, and they found an alternative means of discovering it in the idea of natural law. God revealed his will for mankind partly by direct revelation, as in the Ten Commandments, and partly by endowing every man with the power of reason, which distinguishes him from other animals and, potentially at least, enables him to work out what was God's will for men. Natural law consists of the principles which man's reason dictates. Since this reason is essentially the same among all peoples and in all ages, natural law is similarly universal and unchanging.

GROTIUS AND PUFENDORF

In the first half of the eighteenth century, the most influential writers on natural law were still the Dutchman, Hugo Grotius, whose *De iure belli ac pacis* appeared in 1625, and the German, Samuel Pufendorf, whose *De iure naturae et gentium* was first published in 1672. Both of these works were translated into English[1] and enjoyed much popularity in the late seventeenth and early eighteenth century. Before 1750 there were six editions in English of Grotius' *De iure belli* and four of Pufendorf's *De iure naturae*, while of Pufendorf's shorter work, *De officio hominis et civis iuxta legem naturalem*, no fewer than nine editions of the Latin version, seven editions of the English translation and even one of Barbeyrac's French version were published in Britain between 1682 and 1758.

Grotius and Pufendorf sought to establish the existence of certain universal legal principles which were binding on all men, irrespective of the time and the place in which they lived. They could then be regarded as the basis of an international law. These

---

[1] I have used F. W. Kelsey's translation of *De iure belli* (Oxford, 1925), and C. H. and W. A. Oldfather's translation of *De iure naturae* (Oxford, 1934), both in the 'Classics of International Law' series.

principles were axiomatic. They had the same certainty and generality as a proposition of mathematics, and seventeenth-century writers on natural law frequently invoked the mathematical analogy. They did not, however, think of natural law as covering the whole area of human relations governed by law. The bulk of a particular society's law was not natural but positive, and that differed from one country to another and from one period to another. Because they varied from place to place and were subject to change, the rules of positive law were regarded by Grotius as incapable of systematic treatment. However, the foundation of a society's law, the basic principles, were considered to be governed by natural law.

The principles of natural law could be proved in two ways, either *a posteriori*, that is, empirically by showing that they had been generally accepted as part of the law of nature on the testimony of philosophers, poets and orators through the ages, or *a priori*, by deducing them logically from the unchanging rational and social nature of man.

Grotius concentrated on the empirical approach. We cannot, of course, believe everything the writers of antiquity say, because sometimes their arguments are biassed. But when many writers 'at different times, and in different places, affirm the same thing as certain, that ought to be referred to a universal cause; and this cause...must be either a correct conclusion drawn from the principles of nature, or common consent. The former points to the law of nature; the latter to the law of nations' (*De iure belli*, *prolegomena*, sec. 40). Thus proof *a posteriori* demonstrates 'if not with absolute assurance, at least with every probability, that that is according to the law of nature which is believed to be such among all nations or among all those that are more advanced in civilization' (1.1.12). Grotius' contemporaries generally thought that he rather overdid this approach, by overwhelming his readers with a massive display of erudition.

Pufendorf was uneasy about the notion of discovering the law of nature in the consent of mankind in general or at least in that of the most polished nations. The manners and customs of nations are so varied that we cannot properly know them all and if we try to confine ourselves to the most civilised, how shall we identify which nations they are? What nation is going to admit that it is barbarous? And what nation will set itself up as a standard for others? Innocence and integrity may indeed be more readily found in the less highly polished nations than in the more advanced. The usual practices can easily be mistaken for the dictates of natural reason (*De iure naturae*, II.3.7).

In preference to the *a posteriori* method, Pufendorf concentrated on the accurate contemplation of the nature, condition and desires of man himself (II.3.14). Like every other animal, man is first of all motivated by a desire for self-protection and tries to obtain whatever will benefit him and avoid whatever will harm him. This self-love is, however, combined with a helplessness and an inability to achieve his desires by himself, without the co-operation of his fellow creatures. Once these two basic ideas are accepted, it is, says Pufendorf, easy to deduce the need for society and a natural law governing that society:

It is quite clear that man is an animal extremely desirous of his own preservation, in himself exposed to want, unable to exist without the help of his fellow-creatures, fitted in a remarkable way to contribute to the common good, and yet at all times malicious, petulant and easily irritated, as well as quick and powerful to do injury. For such an animal to live and enjoy the good things that in this world attend his condition, it is necessary that he be sociable, that is, be willing to join himself with others like him, and conduct himself towards them in such a way that, far from having any cause to do him harm, they may feel that there is reason to preserve and increase his good fortune (II.3.15).

In their different ways, both Grotius and Pufendorf were seeking to prove the existence of certain general principles which bound every man by his nature, and which were themselves unchanging. But they did not mean that all legal institutions derived from those principles were always the same. Civil government, property and contracts are institutions found in most communities, but they did not exist in the state of nature. They were introduced as and when they were required to meet man's needs. Nevertheless, man is under an obligation imposed by natural law to respect such institutions. For natural law lays down that in general one should obey the state authorities; that is, unless they order one to contravene the natural law (Grotius, *De iure belli*, 1.4).

In an important passage (*De iure naturae*, IV.4.14), Pufendorf discusses in what sense private property can properly be regarded as an institution of natural law. An institution may be described as part of natural law in two senses; first, because it derives from some principle of natural law that something should be done or not done; and secondly, because it proceeds from some institution suggested by natural law for the better running of society. An institution of natural law in the first sense existed even in the state of nature. An institution in the second sense was introduced because right reason, out of consideration for the condition of social life, had shown the need for it. If it were introduced simply on grounds of expediency, or because it was advantageous to a particular society only, then the institution would be part of positive law. It is the fact that reason demonstrates that all men in a certain condition of society would benefit from its introduction that makes it an institution of natural law. No principle of natural law dictates that there must be private property, so it is not natural in the first sense. It did not exist in the state of nature. But it is natural in the second sense, since it was gradually introduced and accepted in all civilised communities as a necessary institution.

It is the fact that man is a social animal that for Pufendorf explains why he lives in society with others and it is from this fact that he deduces the basic principles of natural law, which apply even in a state of natural liberty. These principles include the obligation to carry out one's promises, on which the obligatory character of a social contract ultimately rests (III.4.2). They also justify the right of the husband over his wife (VI.1.11) and the right of parents over children (VI.2.4). Thus families under a patriarchal head can exist even in a condition of natural liberty, and the biblical patriarchs in Genesis were in such a condition.

If the sociability of man explains society, it does not explain why men set up states and governments. Pufendorf rejects the suggestion that the desire for a better standard of living was the main reason for the establishment of states. Genesis shows that when men were still living scattered about and divided into distinct families, they provided themselves with the necessities of life, having learned agriculture, herding, the culture of the vine, the making of clothing and other arts. The true reason why the patriarchs abandoned natural liberty to set up states was to defend themselves against the attacks of their fellow men. The dominant motive was fear of other men. Respect for the law of nature does not ensure the peace of society. A stronger control was needed, and so the family heads agreed to set up a government (VII.1.3ff.).

At what point the family heads agreed to form a state was a matter of debate. The patriarch of Genesis has 'all the rights of a prince or supreme magistrate in his family, and consequently can make laws, punish delinquents, make war and peace and enter into treaties'; indeed he can exercise all the functions of the sovereign of a state. For the large family groups described in Genesis were really little states in themselves; and the motivation of their heads to set up the apparatus of a large state was not so clear. By the beginning of the eighteenth century even loyal natural lawyers were expressing doubts about the adequacy of Pufendorf's account: J. G. Heineccius in his *Elementa iuris naturae et gentium* asked:

Why might not the more simple societies have produced all the advantages of union, since in these every one was at liberty to acquire what he pleased and there would be none of those tributes, taxes, imposts, upon persons or estates there, which now eat up the property and estates of subjects in civil governments? Let nature be as abhorrent of solitude and let a state of solitude be as miserable as Pufendorff hath painted it out to be, yet we can never say that Abraham, for example, lived in a solitary state, who besides a wife and a handmaid, and many children by both, had such a numerous retinue of servants that he could bring into the field three hundred and eighty servants born in his family, Gen.xiv.13. However strong the natural propensity of mankind to society may be, yet surely they were not immediately led by natural inclination to form those larger societies, in which there are many things contrary to the natural dispositions of mankind, as Pufendorff hath shewn [VII.1.4]. It is however very certain, that in a civil state, if it be rightly constituted, justice is well administered, and all the public and private interests of mankind are wisely consulted and provided for; but those things are more properly called consequences of good civil government, than motive causes to the formation of it.[2]

Both Grotius and Pufendorf describe private property as developing gradually out of a primitive form of community of property, but their accounts of the development were restricted by the need to incorporate data given in the Scriptures. Grotius says that God originally granted a dominion over the things of this world to mankind in general. Had men retained their primitive innocence, this state of things would have lasted. That is proved by the practice of some contemporary American Indians, who are still in this state, and know no private property in land. However, men

[2] 3rd edn (1744), II.6.103, translated by George Turnbull as *A Methodical System of Universal Law* (London, 1763), II.6.102.

began to specialise in particular arts, such as agriculture and the raising of cattle, and this led to mutual envy and ambition. Later, after Babel, land was divided among different nations, but there was still community of pastures among neighbours until growth of population forced a division of lands among families. Gradually the desire for a better life, specialisation of labour, and lack of love for one's fellow men made equality of goods impossible, and so the old community of property gave way to private property. 'This happened not by a mere act of will...but rather by a kind of agreement, either expressed, as by a division, or implied, as by occupation' (*De iure belli*, II.2.21–5).

Pufendorf makes the comment that the early community of property enjoyed by primitive man was not positive community, as it is understood in modern times, which presupposes an explicit notion of property. It was rather negative community, in the sense that there was no notion of property at all, everything being enjoyed in common. If everyone had continued to live in brotherly love, like the early Christians in Jerusalem, or the Essenes described by Philo (both of whom had been cited by Grotius), private property would never have been necessary. But most men are not saints, and their nature leads to a division of property (*De iure naturae*, IV.4.9–10).

Even among the classical natural law writers, therefore, there was a recognition that some of the fundamental institutions of state, the apparatus of government and private property, are not 'original', but appear only when men are ready for them.[3] In Britain the discussion of the subject in the eighteenth century was carried on not by lawyers but by moral philosophers, concerned about the basis of man's duties to his fellow men in society.

---

[3] D. Forbes, *Hume's Philosophical Politics* (Cambridge, 1975), 28: 'it is not a forced or distorted interpretation which points out how, for the natural law writers...government or "civil society" is a purely human expedient which emerges with the development of society to meet human needs, psychological and material'.

HUTCHESON

An important mediator of natural law thinking in English was Francis Hutcheson,[4] who was Professor of Moral Philosophy at Glasgow from 1729 until his death in 1746. He regarded himself as in the tradition of Grotius and Pufendorf, but introduced a new note into the investigation of natural law by stressing the element of empirical observation of man's feelings. Indeed his contemporaries considered that it was he who first applied the inductive method, developed by the natural scientists, or 'natural philosophers', as they were called, in the study of morals. Hutcheson's colleague at Glasgow, William Leechman, explained that in the natural sciences, thinkers had 'thrown off the method of forming hypotheses and suppositions, and had set themselves to make observations and experiments on the constitution of the material world itself'. In the same way, Hutcheson believed, a more exact theory of morals could be reached only 'from proper observations upon the several powers and principles which we are conscious of in our own bosoms', and through a 'more strict philosophical enquiry into the various natural principles or natural dispositions of mankind, in the same way that we enquire into the structure of an animal body, of a plant or of the solar system'. Since 'the moral constitution of our nature' is the work of the Supreme Being, by studying it, we are carrying out His will.[5]

What Hutcheson claimed to be observing was not the way men behaved or actual systems of conduct, but rather man's feelings about conduct. His study was psychological. He believed strongly in the existence of a moral sense which approves what is good and disapproves what is bad, so that the principles of right conduct are discovered from 'the moral determinations of the heart and the

---

[4] Dugald Stewart considered that Hutcheson's lectures 'appear to have contributed very powerfully to diffuse, in Scotland, that taste for analytical discussion, and that spirit of liberal inquiry, to which the world is indebted for some of the most valuable productions of the eighteenth century', *Collected Works* (10 vols., Edinburgh, 1854–60, reprinted Farnborough, 1971), x.82 (cf. also 1.428–9); W. R. Scott, *Francis Hutcheson* (Cambridge, 1900); W. L. Taylor, *Francis Hutcheson and David Hume as Predecessors of Adam Smith* (Durham, N.C., 1965).

[5] Preface to Hutcheson's posthumous *System of Moral Philosophy* (2 vols., London, 1755), xiii–xv.

conclusions of right reason from these determinations' (*System*, 1.269).

Hutcheson wanted to dissociate himself from ethical rationalists, such as Samuel Clarke, whose systems depended exclusively on reason. For Hutcheson, reason was applied only after the natural senses had been examined.

His course in moral philosophy was divided into two parts: 'ethicks' and 'the law of nature', and the latter was subdivided into: '(1) the doctrine of private rights or laws obtaining in natural liberty; (2) Oeconomics, or the laws and rights of the several members of a family; and (3) Politics, showing the various plans of civil government and the rights of states with respect to each others'.[6]

The rights obtaining in natural liberty are indicated by the feelings of our hearts, by our automatic approval of what is of advantage to us and of no harm to others. After observing our natural feelings, we should consider the general interest of society. That will tend to confirm what we have felt. The sense of everyone's heart indicates that everyone has rights to life, to reputation and to personal liberty and these indications are confirmed by considerations of common utility.

Hutcheson makes much of the difference between perfect rights, enforceable in a law court, and imperfect rights, which are recognised by morality but not by law. For him this distinction was more important than that between natural law and positive law. Our feelings make little distinction between the two kinds of rights, but reason recognises the need for making it. Hutcheson likens the broad intuitive approach of the feelings to the revealed rules found in the Scriptures. In each case reason has to supply the fine tuning which distinguishes perfect from imperfect rights. Thus we are told 'thou shalt not kill'; it is not, however, all killing which is prohibited, but only murder; and only reason can tell us what killings amount to murder and what do not. So also with the admonition, 'thou shalt not steal': ''Tis our reason again must teach us the origin, the nature, and extent of property; and it will shew us too that property must often give place to some great publick interests.' Again, 'lye not to each other' is a general rule

[6] *Short Introduction to Moral Philosophy* (Glasgow, 1753), v.

approved by all. It is our reason which shows 'what sort of speech hurts society and what not', and when there is justification for receding from the general rule of telling the truth (*System*, II.130–1). Hutcheson's separation of what the heart approves and what reason provides led him to be very conscious of the limitations of the legal process.

When he deals with the obligation of promises, he argues that between the category of mere statements of future intention, which do not bind at all, and that of fully binding contracts, is an intermediate class of promises,

> when we promise something for the advantage of another, expecting his dependence on our promise and yet not designing to convey to him any right to compel us to observe it... Receding from such promises without a just cause is very faulty in point of veracity and must be highly disapproved by every honest heart on that very account – as well as the cruelty and inhumanity sometimes displayed in defeating the just hopes we had raised by another's dependence on our veracity... But when one departs from such a promise, the other party has no other perfect right than to demand compensation of any damage he sustained by taking his measures in dependence on the promise.

The promisee enjoys such a right only if the measures he has taken are justifiable and he has given no cause to the promisor for departing from his promise. He 'cannot, even so, compel the performance of the promise' (*System*, II.5–6).

Hutcheson felt that earlier writers, such as Hobbes, had exaggerated the disadvantages of a pre-political society. Man in the state of nature was not a solitary being fighting for survival against everyone else, but was part of a large family unit, in which there could be much happiness and even improvement of the arts. He investigates at length how controversies should be decided in natural liberty (*System*, II.141–7) and concludes that they would be submitted to an arbitrator, chosen by the parties, to whom they must submit the dispute absolutely. This arbitrator would hear the evidence of witnesses, and would follow the rule that to prove any matter the evidence of at least two witnesses is needed. In general, however, civil society, formed by a social contract, was preferable to the anarchy of natural liberty, since any society which has advanced beyond the primitive state needs a more effective administration of justice than can be obtained in natural liberty (*System*, II.214–25).

Hutcheson himself showed little interest in the manner of development of legal institutions. But in two ways he prepared the way for later Scottish thinkers to direct their attention to it. First, by stressing the importance of other men's sense of approval and disapproval in determining the rightness and wrongness of conduct and the need to submit disputes to 'unbiassed arbitrators' (*System*, 1.328), he opened the way for later writers to show that such approval and disapproval were not constant among all people but changed as attitudes changed from one society to another.

Secondly, by stressing the difference between what one ought morally to do and what one can be compelled legally to do, Hutcheson directed the attention of thinkers away from ideal systems to actual legal systems, to the differences between them and to the reasons for those differences.

HUME

A further step away from the traditional natural law thinking was taken by David Hume[7] in his *Treatise of Human Nature*, published in 1740. For Hume the state of nature was a fiction, and society did not come into existence through the conscious, rational method of contract. The very idea of a social contract was far beyond the comprehension of the savages who lived in a pre-political condition. What happened was rather that men living on their own gradually came to recognise the benefits of living together in communities. Once they had formed a society, men could achieve more and be more secure than was possible when they were on their own. 'By the conjunction of forces, our power is augmented: By the partition of employments, our ability encreases: And by mutual succour we are less expos'd to fortune and accidents.' As a result, man in society is 'in every respect more satisfied and happy, than 'tis possible for him, in his savage and solitary condition, ever to become' (*Treatise*, 485).

Having set out the benefits of living in society, Hume points out

[7] H. C. Cairns, *Legal Philosophy from Plato to Hegel* (Baltimore, 1949), 362–89; F. A. Hayek, 'The legal and political philosophy of David Hume', *Studies in Philosophy, Politics and Economics* (London, 1967), 106–21; Forbes, *Hume's Philosophical Politics*. I have used L. A. Selby-Bigge's editions of the *Treatise* (Oxford, 1888) and of the *Enquiry* (Oxford, 1902).

the obstacles which prevent those benefits from being fully realised. They are the facts, recognised already by Pufendorf, first, that men are selfish and have only limited generosity, and secondly, that there are not enough goods in the world to satisfy everyone's desires. 'If men were supplied with every thing in the same abundance, or if *every one* had the same affection and tender regard for *every one* as for himself; justice and injustice would be equally unknown among mankind.' Consequently, it is 'only from the selfishness and confin'd generosity of men, along with the scanty provision nature has made for his wants, that justice derives its origin' (*Treatise*, 495).

If it were not for these factors, societies would not need laws. As it is, the circumstances of living together in society give rise to three fundamental laws, namely those 'of the stability of possession, of its transference by consent and of the performance of promises' (*Treatise*, 526). It is on the strict observance of these laws of property that the peace and security of society depend. 'The convention for the distinction of property, and for the stability of possession, is of all circumstances the most necessary to the establishment of human society' (*Treatise*, 491).

Hume calls the recognition of these rules a convention but it 'is not of the nature of a *promise*'; rather it is 'a general sense of common interest', by which men gradually become conscious of the need to regulate their conduct according to rules. The convention about stability of possession 'arises gradually, and acquires force by a slow progression, and by our repeated experience of the inconveniences of transgressing it' (*Treatise*, 490). It is from these conventions that ideas of justice and injustice are derived. They emerge like a language or the recognition of gold and silver as a measure of exchange. Thus Hume's view is that ideas of property, language and money are all human conventions which have developed gradually and come to be accepted by habit and practice.

Since justice is entirely concerned with property, it must itself be the product of man's artifice rather than of nature. Hume does, however, consider that ideas of property and justice are universal, so that it is quite proper to call them natural. 'Tho' the rules of justice be *artificial*, they are not *arbitrary*. Nor is the expression improper to call them *Laws of Nature*; if by natural we understand what is common to any species, or even if we confine it to mean what is inseparable from the species' (*Treatise*, 484).

In his *Enquiry concerning the Principles of Morals* (1751), Hume developed the argument that the origin of justice is public utility and 'that reflections on the beneficial consequences of this virtue are the *sole* foundation of its merit' (p. 183). In a situation of abundance, where everyone has more than enough to satisfy his desires, or in a situation where everyone is so friendly and generous 'that every man has the utmost tenderness for every man, and feels no more concern for his own interest than for that of his fellows' (*Enquiry*, 185), there would be no need for property, and the notion of justice would be useless. So also in cases of dire necessity, the strict laws of justice are suspended and give way to the desire for self-preservation. The justification of property being utility, 'by rendering justice totally *useless*, you thereby totally destroy its essence and suspend its obligation upon mankind' (*Enquiry*, 188). The conclusion is that 'the rules of equity or justice depend entirely on the particular state and condition in which men are placed' (*ibid.*).

Questions concerning property are determined by civil laws which conform with the particular convenience of each community. Often, in order that we can determine the objects of property,

> we must have recourse to statutes, customs, precedents, analogies and a hundred other circumstances; some of which are constant and inflexible, some variable and arbitrary. But the ultimate point, in which they all professedly terminate, is the interest and happiness of human society. Where this enters not into consideration, nothing can appear more whimsical, unnatural, and even superstitious, than all or most of the laws of justice and of property (*Enquiry*, 197–8).

Like Hutcheson, Hume did not concern himself expressly with the process of legal change, but by stressing the gradual way in which men by force of habit come to accept certain conventions about property, which are justified by their utility in that particular society, he helped to create a climate of opinion in which ideas of legal evolution could emerge. In particular he brought out the point that institutions which are necessary for a civilised and orderly society may not have been created with that end in view. They are institutions 'advantagous to the public, tho'...not intended for that purpose by the inventors' (*Treatise*, 529).

MONTESQUIEU

Hume's ideas on the character of legal institutions and their gradual development were part of a much larger investigation of human nature. Although he set them out clearly enough, his account was abstract in the sense that, except in his treatment of the methods of acquisition of ownership, when he referred to Roman law in some detail, he did not relate them to specific legal systems. His ideas made less impact on thinking about legal change that those of his French contemporary, Baron Montesquieu. His *De l'esprit des lois* appeared in 1748, eight years after the publication of Hume's *Treatise*, and was soon translated into English.[8] Montesquieu provided examples galore to illustrate the connection of law with the circumstances of society, and indeed it is sometimes not easy to extract his precise ideas from the mass of detail in which he has buried them.

To those familiar with the natural law tradition Montesquieu did not, at first sight, seem to be so radical. For he begins with the reassuring observation that 'laws, in their most general signification, are the necessary relations arising from the nature of things' (1.1). Each category of being, God, the material world, beasts and men, has its own laws. What distinguishes men from other beings is reason, which is common to all men, and human law 'in general is human reason, inasmuch as it governs all the inhabitants of the earth' (1.3). So the actual legal systems of particular nations are the particular applications of human reason. At this point, however, Montesquieu points out that, though reason may be unchanging, it has to be applied to different situations in different societies. The nature of things is not the same from one society to another, and reason cannot ignore the difference.

> The political and civil laws of each nation...should be adapted in such a manner to the people for whom they are framed, that it is a great chance if those of one nation suit another. They should be relative to the nature and principle of each government...They should be relative to the climate of each country, to the quality of its soil, to its situation and extent, to the principal occupation of the natives, whether husbandmen, huntsmen or shepherds; they should have a relation to the degree of liberty which the constitution will bear: to the religion of the inhabitants, to their inclinations, riches, numbers, commerce, manners and customs. In fine, they have relations to each other, as also to their origin, to the

---

[8] Translated by T. Nugent (2 vols., London, 1752): I have used the 1823 edition.

intent of the legislator, and to the order of things on which they are established; in all which different lights they ought to be considered...all these [relations] together constitute what I call the *Spirit of Laws* (1.3).

Montesquieu recognised that laws are not the only kind of norm governing societies. Religion, customs, manners, political tradition, also control a person's conduct in society, and each kind of norm is connected with the others. Together they dictate the general spirit of a nation. Montesquieu's treatise contains many examples, taken both from the writers of classical antiquity and from contemporary travel writers, to illustrate this basic thesis. The point is that laws ought to reflect differences in societies and they are good laws in proportion to the extent to which they do take them into account.

For example, he explains that in hot climates women mature early and they become attractive to men long before their intellects have matured. 'Their reason therefore never accompanies their beauty.' In such climates, wives will marry young and perforce be in a state of dependence to their husbands, and polygamy will be allowed. In temperate climates, on the other hand, women mature later, they have children when they are older and so they have more reason and knowledge at the time of their marriage. There is more equality between the sexes and the law can require monogamy (XVI.2).

It should now be clear that the subject of Montesquieu's treatise is not the same as that of the natural law writers. They were primarily concerned with the basic laws which obtained in a state of natural liberty, before political society had come into being. He is concerned more with the law of developed societies, which already have some form of government. He dismisses natural law in one page (1.2), and concentrates on positive law. His aim is to guide legislators in the task of making good laws, and good is not something abstract but what is good for their particular societies. Montesquieu is not an environmental determinist. He envisages positive laws as mainly formulated by legislators, who are admittedly limited in what they can appropriately do by the political organisation, physical conditions, religion and so on of their people, but who can nonetheless impress their own character on the laws they enact.

Montesquieu recognised that laws must change and in some

passages he seems to contemplate a cyclical form of change. But he was vague as to the process of change and did not offer any scheme of legal development. *De l'esprit des lois* is remarkable for its emphasis on the particular, the concrete, and it is this feature which, in part at least, accounted for its popularity. The work shifted the focus of legal speculation from the rules that governed men naturally, irrespective of the society in which they lived, to the rules which actually existed as specific phenomena in specific societies, past and present. He related differences in law to differences in the social and economic conditions of society, but he did not project those differences on to an historical plane. He did not relate ancient societies to modern societies nor did he suggest that all societies pass through recognisable stages of development. He was, in fact, reluctant to attribute large relationships of cause and effect too readily. Thus discussing the importance of commerce, he says: 'I am not ignorant that men prepossessed with these two ideas, that commerce is of the greatest service to a state, and that the Romans had the best regulated government in the world, have believed that these people greatly honoured and encouraged commerce; but the truth is, they seldom troubled their heads about it' (XXI.14).

Montesquieu's failure to develop the similarity between certain ancient societies and contemporary savage societies was not a failure to anticipate what later writers would soon be saying. A writer who had made detailed comparisons between the habits and customs of the American Indians and those of the ancient Greeks, was J.-F. Lafitau, like Montesquieu a citizen of Bordeaux, whose *Moeurs des sauvages Amériquains comparées aux moeurs des premiers temps*,[9] was published in 1724. Yet Montesquieu never cites him. Previous writers had tended to treat the American Indians as savages and nothing more. Lafitau, a Jesuit missionary who spent many years among the Iroquois, was struck by the similarity of certain Indian customs to those he had read about in classical writings. He states that he was not satisfied with learning about Indian ways and scoured classical literature for evidence of the customs of primitive peoples which he could compare with those

[9] Edited and translated by W. N. Fenton and E. L. Moore, Champlain Society (2 vols., Toronto, 1974), I.

that he had observed in America. He marshalled an array of data drawn both from classical literature and from contemporary travellers, which illustrated the similarity of the customs of the New World and those reported on the fringes of the ancient world. He regarded the similarity as so striking and the customs as so distinctive that they could only be explained on the basis of a common origin. In his view the New World was populated from the Old across Asia.

The significance of Lafitau's work is best brought out in his own words:

I confess that if the ancient authors have given me information on which to base happy conjectures about the Indians, the customs of the Indians have given me information on the basis of which I can understand more easily and explain more readily many things in the ancient authors. Perhaps, by bringing my thoughts to light, I shall open to those interested in the reading of these authors some paths of investigation that they will be able to follow further.

For Homer's Odyssey was an essay in the science of the manners and customs of different peoples (1.27). Lafitau's book, in Professor A. D. Momigliano's words, by setting Greek and Iroquois customs side by side, 'revealed to the world the simple truth that also the Greeks had once been savages'.[10]

Montesquieu may have been prejudiced against Lafitau on religious grounds.[11] If that is so, there were others who soon used Lafitau's 'simple truth' to make an important advance on Montesquieu's own ideas. He was well aware, of course, that some societies and their laws were primitive and others advanced, but he did not try to explain the conditions which govern why some societies progress and others do not. Given the multiplicity of factors which he identified as the components of a society's spirit, it would have been difficult for him to offer such an explanation without giving some of those factors greater prominence than others, and that he seemed reluctant to do.

The interest provoked by Montesquieu's work led thinkers to speculate about the source of the differences between one society and another, which he had set out so excitingly, and the decade following the publication of *De l'esprit des lois* saw a concentration of attention on one of the factors to which he had referred, namely,

[10] *Studies in Historiography* (London, 1966), 141.
[11] Lafitau, edn of Fenton and Moore, lxxxiii and xciii.

the mode of subsistence. At the beginning of his book, when listing the factors of which the laws must take account, Montesquieu mentioned 'the principal occupation of the natives, whether husbandmen, huntsmen or shepherds' (1.3). Later he proclaims, 'The laws have a very great relation to the manner in which the several nations procure their subsistence. There should be a code of laws of a much larger extent for a nation attached to trade and navigation, than for a people who are content with cultivating the earth. There should be a much greater for the latter than for those who subsist by flocks and herds. There must be a still greater for these, than for such as live by hunting' (XVIII.8).

Two groups of thinkers, one in France and the other in Scotland, in prosecuting the search for the pattern of legal origins, developed these remarks in two ways. First, they treated the mode of subsistence as not merely one of several factors affecting the character of a society's laws but as the crucial circumstance which dictated their nature and scope; and secondly, they reversed the order of Montesquieu's remarks and converted them into a scheme of development applicable to primitive societies generally.

As a result the theory was propounded that early societies pass through certain stages of development, at first three and then four in number, namely, hunting, pastoral, agricultural and commercial.

Professor R. L. Meek[12] has set out the evidence for the appearance of the four-stage theory in detail. So far as French thinkers were concerned, he argues that it was first enunciated by Turgot in his *De l'histoire universelle*, a work written about 1751–2, but not published until after its author's death.

GOGUET

The earliest French work to contain a statement of the theory in relation to (among other things) the progress of law in society – also incidentally one of the earliest actually to publish the theory – was Antoine Yves Goguet's *De l'origine des lois, des arts, et des sciences, et de leurs progrès chez les anciens peuples*,[13] published in

---

[12] Meek, *Social Science and the Ignoble Savage* (Cambridge, 1976), 68ff.

[13] Translated by Henry, Dunn and Spearman (3 vols., Edinburgh, 1761); Meek, *Social Science*, 94ff.

1758. The author, who was a lawyer and councillor of the Parlement de Paris, died of smallpox in the same year, at the age of forty-two. His work excited considerable interest and, since an English translation was published in Edinburgh in 1761, it provides a link between the French and Scottish thinkers on the subject. Goguet offers a highly systematic account of developments from the Flood until the accession of Cyrus to the throne of Persia, concentrating mainly on the Babylonians, Hebrews, Egyptians, and Greeks, but with many references to other nations, such as Indians and Chinese, and to contemporary savage societies. It is divided into three parts, corresponding to historical periods, the first ending with the death of Jacob and the second with the establishment of monarchy among the Israelites. Each part is divided into six sections, dealing respectively with laws and government, arts and manufactures, sciences, commerce and navigation, the 'art-military', and manners and customs.

In the preface Goguet criticises earlier writers for 'indulging themselves too much in conjectures, by following fancies more than facts and taking their own imaginations, rather than the lights of history, for their guides', and promises that he will be more true to history (p. v). By implication he suggests that he will be more comprehensive, more historical and more systematic than Montesquieu.

'My design has been to display the whole mass of knowledge of all kinds among each people, in each age...to make us sensible of the difference between one nation and another at the same time, and in the same nation at different times in all those various branches of knowledge' (p. ix). For 'the arts especially, bear so strong an impression of the people by whom they have been cultivated, that an attentive examination of their origin and progress is the most effectual way to discover the genius, the manners and turn of mind, of the various nations in the world' (p. v).

Although pledged to avoid conjecture as far as possible, Goguet admits that with regard to the earliest period he sometimes found himself 'destitute of facts and historical monuments'. In explaining what he did in that situation he seems to echo Lafitau, and his statement of method is worth repeating in full:

I consulted what has been said, both by ancient and modern writers, on the manners of savage nations. I imagined that the conduct of these nations would give us pretty clear and just ideas of the state of the first wandering colonies, immediately after the confusion of tongues and dispersion of families. We may collect both from ancient and modern relations of this kind, several points of comparison, capable of removing many doubts which might arise about certain extraordinary facts, which I have thought proper to build upon. The relations concerning America in particular, have been extremely useful to me on this article. We may judge of the state of the ancient world for some time after the deluge, by the condition of the greatest part of the new world when it was first discovered. In comparing what the first adventurers have told us concerning America, with what antiquity has transmitted to us concerning the manner in which the inhabitants of our continent lived in those times which were reckoned the first ages of the world, we cannot but perceive the most evident and striking resemblance and conformity. I have, therefore, pretty often compared the relations of modern travellers with those of ancient historians, and intermingled their narrations, with a design to support the testimony of ancient writers, to shew the possibility, and even reality of certain facts which they relate, and certain customs which they mention. These different passages thus compared and brought together, mutually support each other, and lay a solid foundation for every thing I have said concerning the progress of the human understanding, in its improvements and discoveries, which I date from the deluge. For...whatever knowledge mankind had acquired before that time, was almost entirely lost in that terrible desolation (pp. xiv–xv).

In dealing with the origin of laws and government, Goguet distinguishes between laws essential to any society, however undeveloped, and those peculiar to a society which follows agriculture.

There was a time, when mankind derived their whole subsistence from the fruits which the earth produced spontaneously, from their hunting, fishing, and their flocks. This kind of life obliged them often to change their abode, consequently they had no dwelling place nor settled habitations. Such was the ancient manner of living, till agriculture was introduced; in this manner several nations still live, as the Scythians, Tartars, Arabians, Savages etc.

The discovery of agriculture introduced a different set of manners. Those nations who applied to that art, were obliged to fix in a certain district. They built and inhabited cities. This kind of society having need of many more arts than were necessary for those who neglected or were ignorant of agriculture, must of consequence need also many more laws (pp. 16–17).

Among the laws required even by societies without agriculture are rights of property in moveables, marriage ceremonies, and penal laws. An agricultural society needs in addition rules relating to property in land, inheritances, in fact the bulk of what we call civil law. 'Agriculture...gave birth to the greatest part of the arts, arts produced commerce, and commerce necessarily occasioned a great number of regulations: it even became necessary, in succeeding times, to extend or reform these regulations in proportion as commerce grew more extensive' (p. 33).

So far, although singling out the introduction of agriculture as the key to the development of civil laws, Goguet has not indicated any 'stages' of development of societies. Later, however, when discussing the development of arts, he offers a scheme of development.

> In some countries they would begin by improvements in the arts of hunting and fishing. Hunting especially, was the principal employment of a great part of mankind in the first ages of the world. They were obliged to this in order to defend their own lives against the assaults of wild beasts, as well as to procure subsistence. There are still a great many nations in both continents, whose whole employment is hunting and fishing.
>
> But the more industrious and discerning part of mankind would soon observe, that amongst that innumerable multitude of animals which were spread over the face of the earth, there were some which lived in droves and herds, and were much more tame and tractable than the rest. They would endeavour to make themselves masters of these, to confine them in inclosures, to make them multiply that they might always have a sufficient number of them at their command. A great part of the world in these first ages, and for a long time after, derived their chief subsistence from their flocks. We know several numerous and powerful nations who at this day follow this way of life, and are furnished with every thing they stand in need of from their flocks and herds.
>
> Men would next apply themselves to examine the productions of the earth. This, without any cultivation, presented them with a great many plants and fruits which afforded very agreeable and substantial nourishment. They would begin their observations upon these, by distinguishing the best kinds, especially such as kept longest after they were gathered. They would next endeavour to find out the best ways of using them, to discover the arts of increasing their quantity and improving their qualities by cultivation. It is to the discovery of agriculture we are indebted for that prodigious number of arts and sciences we now enjoy (pp. 84–5).

The future elaboration of these remarks was made not in France but in Scotland.

2

Scottish philosophical history of law

Goguet showed that the materials collected by Montesquieu could be so arranged as to suggest a scheme of development. A similar discovery was being made simultaneously in Scotland by a group of thinkers, who applied it more specifically to law. This group was gathered about the genial figure of Henry Home, who in 1752 became a judge of the Court of Session with the title of Lord Kames.[1] It included among its members David Hume (a distant relation of Kames himself), Adam Smith and John Millar. They had been introduced to Montesquieu's *Spirit of the Laws* immediately after its publication, for the author had himself sent a copy to Hume, who helped to publish in Edinburgh a translation of some sections of the work, with the author's latest corrections.[2]

DALRYMPLE AND KAMES

The earliest published work to mention the four stages of society based on modes of subsistence appeared in 1757, the year before Goguet's work was published in France. This was *An Essay towards a General Theory of Feudal Property in Great Britain*,[3] by John Dalrymple of Cranstoun, a young man of thirty-one, who had been admitted advocate in 1748. Its purpose was to trace the progress of the land laws of England and of Scotland, so far as they had a feudal origin; 'to mark their variations in different ages and

---

[1] P. Stein, 'Law and Society in Eighteenth-Century Scottish Thought', in *Scotland in the Age of Improvement*, ed. N. T. Phillipson and R. Mitchison (Edinburgh, 1970), 148–68.
[2] E. C. Mossner, *Life of David Hume* (Edinburgh, 1954), 229.
[3] I have used the 4th edition (London, 1759); cf. Meek, *Social Science and the Ignoble Savage* (Cambridge, 1976), 99–102.

to assign the causes of those variations' (p. vii). It had a political as well as a scholarly motive. 'Such a progress is the more to be attended to, because until the subjects of England and Scotland have a knowledge of each other's laws, there never will be a perfect union of the two kingdoms' (p. viii). Dalrymple's models were the *Spirit of the Laws* and the *Considerations on the Law of Forfeiture* (1745) by Charles Yorke, the son of Lord Chancellor Hardwicke, with whom Kames corresponded on the subject of possible unification of Scots law and English law. These two works showed for the first time 'that it was possible to unite philosophy and history with jurisprudence, and to write even upon a subject of law like a scholar and a gentleman' (p. ix).

Dalrymple dedicated his book to Kames, who had led him 'into the general train of enquiry contained in' it, and claimed that many of the thoughts in it were 'revised by the greatest genius of our age' (Montesquieu). Since Montesquieu died in February 1755, some drafts of the *Essay* must have existed by then.

The stages of society appear as an introduction to the history of the alienation of property in land (ch. III).

The first state of society is that of hunters and fishers; among such a people the idea of property will be confined to a few, and but a very few moveables; and subjects which are immoveable will be esteemed to be common (p. 76).

American tribes may wander hundreds of miles in search of game.

The next state of society begins, when the inconveniences and dangers of such a life lead men to the discovery of pasturage. During this period as soon as a flock has brouzed upon one spot of ground, their proprietors will remove them to another: and the place they have quitted will fall to the next who pleases to take possession of it. For this reason such shepherds will have no notion of property in immoveables, nor of right of possession longer than the act of possession lasts (*ibid.*).

As Lord Stair, the Scottish institutional writer – and incidentally an ancestor of Dalrymple – had pointed out, the lands which the patriarchs in Genesis enjoyed are called their *possessions* (not their property).

A third state of society is produced, when men become so numerous, that the flesh and milk of their cattle is insufficient for their subsistence, and when their more extended intercourse with each other has made them strike out new arts of life and particularly the art of agriculture. This art leading men to bestow thought and labour on land, increases their connection with a single portion of it; this connection long continued, produces an affection; and this affection long continued, together with the other, produces the notion of property in land (p. 77).

Dalrymple confines himself to three 'states' and although he mentions the importance of commerce in improving the standard of life, he does not identify a specific 'state' of commerce.

We have seen that it was precisely in regard to the notion of property that the natural lawyers came nearest to postulating a scheme of legal development, and that it had become almost a commonplace to refer to the American Indians as representatives of a hunting people and to the Biblical patriarchs as representing a pastoral people. Earlier writers, however, thought of hunters and shepherds and even farmers as alternative types of society that might exist among different peoples, and had not suggested that they form a natural progression of stages through which societies generally pass.

Dalrymple confined his statement of the stages of society to property in land and may not have been aware of its potentialities. A year later Kames' *Historical Law Tracts* related the development of law to the development of society in a more systematic way. Kames' work, like Dalrymple's, was written with a view to promoting the unification of English law and Scots law.

Already in his sixties, Kames wrote with great confidence and authority.[4] His aim in all his legal writings was to show that law was not just a 'mass of naked propositions...rarely connected either with premise or consequences', but rather a rational science comparable to moral philosophy (*Elucidations*, vii–x). In his view 'events and subordinate incidents are linked together and connected in a regular chain of causes and effects. Law in particular becomes then only a rational study, when it is traced historically, from its first rudiments among savages, through successive changes, to its highest improvements in a civilized society' (*Law Tracts*, I.v). Montesquieu had opened men's eyes to the necessity of explaining legal institutions in terms of their relation with the circumstances

---

[4] *Historical Law Tracts* (2 vols., Edinburgh, 1758); *Elucidations respecting the Law of Scotland* (Edinburgh, 1777); cf. I. S. Ross, *Lord Kames and the Scotland of his Day* (Oxford, 1972), 202–21; W. C. Lehmann, *Henry Home, Lord Kames, and the Scottish Enlightenment* (The Hague, 1971), 177–215; Meek, *Social Science*, 102–7.

of society. But his work was not historical in that he did not postulate a scheme of development. Kames felt that Montesquieu's approach had limitations. 'That celebrated writer abounds with observations no less pleasing than solid. But a spritely genius, prone to novelty and refinement, has betrayed him into manifold errors' (*Elucidations*, xii). So also, David Hume said of Montesquieu's work that it 'abounds in ingenious and brilliant thoughts, and is not wanting in solidity' He added, however, that in proposing a system according to which all right is 'founded on certain rapports or relations', he was offering a system that 'never will be reconciled with true philosophy' (*Enquiry*, 197 n.).

As Mr Duncan Forbes[5] has pointed out, the *Spirit of the Laws* lacked an organising principle around which its author's observations on law and society could be organised. The Scottish thinkers supplied the deficiency in the principle relating law to the progress of society from barbarism to civilisation. One of the topics discussed by Kames, as it was also at the same time engaging the attention of Goguet, was Egyptian criminal law and its connection with the special physical position of the country. It struck him that the river Nile was a metaphor for law itself.

When we enter upon the municipal law of any country in its present state we resemble a traveller, who crossing the Delta, loses his way among the numberless branches of the Egyptian river. But when we begin at the source and follow the current of law...all its relations and dependencies are traced with no greater difficulty, than are the many streams into which that magnificent river is divided before it is lost in the sea (*Law Tracts*, 1.ix–x).

If Kames' first aim was to be historical, his second was to be comparative, to set the institutions of one legal system against similar institutions in another legal system and account for the differences by reference to the social or cultural differences of the respective societies. For when he spoke of treating law historically, Kames did not mean in an antiquarian way with precise details of legal forms and ceremonies but without any explanation of their origin or purpose or reference to similar ceremonies elsewhere. History meant systematic analysis, comparison and explanation, as in the term 'natural history' for biology.

Kames' history was also philosophical in the sense that he

[5] 'Scientific Whiggism: Adam Smith and John Millar', *Cambridge Journal*, 7 (1954), 646ff.

emphasised causal relations and continuities. Such was his desire to present the history of law as a coherent pattern, that he did not confine himself to what was known about the earliest stages of law. In a similar way to Goguet, whose work appeared in the same year, he justified his method at length in *Historical Law Tracts*:

> In tracing the history of law through dark ages unprovided with records, or so slenderly provided, as not to afford any regular historical chain, we must endeavour, the best way we can, to supply the broken links, by hints from poets and historians, by collateral facts, and by cautious conjecture drawn from the nature of the government, of the people, and of the times. If we use all the light that is afforded, and if the conjectural facts correspond with the few facts that are distinctly vouched, and join all in one regular chain, nothing further can be expected from human endeavours. The evidence is compleat, so far at least as to afford conviction, if it be the best of the kind. This apology is necessary with regard to the subject under consideration. In tracing the history of the criminal law, we must not hope that all the steps and changes can be drawn from the archives of any one nation. In fact, many steps were taken, and many changes made, before archives were kept, and even before writing was a common art. We must be satisfied with collecting the facts and circumstances as they may be gathered from the laws of different countries; and if these put together make a regular system of causes and effects, we may rationally conclude that the progress has been the same among all nations, in the capital circumstances at least; for accidents, or the singular nature of a people or of a government, will always produce some peculiarities (1.36–7).

More historical than Hutcheson or Hume in his approach to legal institutions, Kames followed them in their stress on psychological factors. In his essay on property, he applies the three stages, as Dalrymple had done, observing that the forms of ownership are relatively simple during the stages of hunting and pastoralism and develop complexity only in the agricultural stage. Later he launches a sharp attack on 'the violent and unnatural system' of feudal law which was an interruption of man's progress, in that it countered his 'love of independency and property, the most steady and industrious of all human appetites' (1.198).

The system of entails, in particular, is motivated by strong psychological considerations, which Kames enthusiastically exposes:

> We thirst after opulence; and are not satisfied with the full enjoyment of the goods of fortune, unless it be also in our power to give them a perpetual existence, and to preserve them for ever to ourselves and our families. This purpose, we are conscious, cannot be fully accomplished; but we approach to it as near as we can, by the aid of imagination. The man who has amassed great wealth, cannot think

of quitting his hold; and yet alas! he must die and leave the enjoyment to others. To colour a dismal prospect, he makes a deed, arresting fleeting property, securing his estate to himself and to those who represent him in endless...succession. His estate and his heirs must for ever bear his name; every thing to perpetuate his memory and his wealth. How unfit for the frail condition of mortals are such swoln conceptions! The feudal system unluckily suggested a hint for gratifying this irrational appetite (1.217–18).

So also in his essay on the development of criminal law, Kames relates it to the passion of resentment of the victim of injury and his desire for revenge. The intervention of society in settling disputes was slower in the case of crimes than in civil disputes since 'revenge, the darling privilege of human nature is never tamely given up' (1.30–1). Here also he applies the three stages of society. In this context he maintains that the 'progressive changes' from hunting and fishing through the shepherd life to agriculture 'may be traced in all nations so far as we have any remains of their original history' (1.77). Pointing out that hunting is the way of a society of single families and pastoralism of an only slightly more complex society, he continues,

The true spirit of society, which consists in mutual benefits, and in making the industry of individuals profitable to others as well as to themselves, was not known till agriculture was invented. Agriculture requires the aid of many other arts. The carpenter, the blacksmith, the mason, and other artificers contribute to it...The intimate union among a multitude of individuals, occasioned by agriculture, discovered a number of social duties, formerly unknown. These behoved to be ascertained by laws, the observance of which must be enforced by punishment. Such operations cannot be carried on, otherwise than by lodging power in one or more persons, to direct the resolutions, and apply the force of the whole society. In short it may be laid down as an universal maxim, that in every society, the advances of government towards perfection, are strictly proportioned to the advances of the society towards intimacy of union.

Stressing that 'it was agriculture which first produced a regular system of government', Kames then shows that the special situation of the Egyptians in the Nile Delta must have required that agriculture, advanced government and perfection of laws should be 'coeval with the peopling of the country' (1.78–80).

The essay on promises and covenants is of interest in that Kames, having previously introduced three stages of society, there suggests a fourth. For 'the invention of agriculture produced to the industrious a superfluity, with which foreign necessaries were purchased'. The resulting rise of commerce increased the need for rules regulating contracts (1.92–3).

Kames' influence on the thinkers of the Scottish enlightenment was as a man of ideas, who stimulated, encouraged and criticised others to test and apply them rather than work out their implications for himself. The range of his interests was encyclopedic, including moral philosophy, literary criticism, and agriculture, as well as law, and he made a substantial contribution to the practical development of Scots law by his judicial work. In his efforts to make law a 'philosophical subject', he was not entirely successful; he was sometimes too removed from reality for the lawyer and too technical for the philosopher. In a letter to Adam Smith, written in 1759, David Hume wrote, 'I am afraid of Kames' *Law Tracts*. A man might as well think of making a fine sauce by a mixture of wormwood and aloes as an agreeable combination by joining metaphysics and Scotch law.'[6] Kames' achievement was to interest his friends in the problems of the law and its development.

ADAM SMITH

Although Dalrymple and Kames were the first actually to publish the theory that legal development is related to the mode of subsistence of society, which passes through certain well-defined stages, it is probable that another member of their salon, namely Adam Smith, had contributed more than either of them to the making of the theory.[7] He had given lectures on the progress of society, under the auspices of Kames and others, in Edinburgh in the years following his return to Scotland after more than six years

---

[6] Quoted by W. F. Tytler (Lord Woodhouselee), *Memoirs of the Life and Writings of Lord Kames*, 2nd edn (3 vols., Edinburgh, 1814), 1.318.

[7] The literature stimulated by the bicentenary of the *Wealth of Nations* in 1976 is enormous; cf. the survey by H. C. Recktenwald, 'An Adam Smith Renaissance, anno 1976?', *Journal of Economic Literature*, 16 (1978), 56–83; D. Winch, *Adam Smith's Politics* (Cambridge, 1978); *Essays on Adam Smith*, ed. A. S. Skinner and T. Wilson (Oxford, 1975); and the Glasgow Edition of the *Works* (used here): *Theory of Moral Sentiments*, ed. D. D. Raphael and A. L. Macfie (Oxford, 1976); *Wealth of Nations*, ed. R. H. Campbell, A. S. Skinner and W. B. Todd (2 vols., Oxford, 1976); and *Lectures on Jurisprudence*, ed. R. L. Meek, D. D. Raphael and P. G. Stein (Oxford, 1978), on which see P. Stein, 'Adam Smith's Theory of Law and Society', *Classical Influences on Western Thought, 1650–1870*, ed. R. R. Bolgar (Cambridge, 1979), 263–73.

in Oxford. The ideas adumbrated in those Edinburgh lectures were then elaborated when he was appointed to the Chair of Moral Philosophy at Glasgow – that earlier occupied by his own teacher Hutcheson – in 1752. Like Hutcheson, Smith dealt first with ethics, and then with 'that part of morality which relates to justice'. John Millar, a student of Smith in his early years at Glasgow, and later his colleague, described this part of his lectures as follows:

> Upon this subject he followed the plan that seems to be suggested by Montesquieu; endeavouring to trace the gradual progress of jurisprudence, both public and private, from the rudest to the most refined ages, and to point out the effect of those arts which contribute to subsistence, and to the accumulation of property, in producing correspondent improvements or alterations in law and government.[8]

At the end of the *Theory of Moral Sentiments*, Smith's first major published work, which appeared in 1759, he announced his intention to produce 'an account of the general principles of law and government, and of the different revolutions they have undergone in the different ages and periods of society, not only in what concerns justice, but in what concerns police, revenue, and arms, and whatever else is the object of law' (p. 342). Although Smith allowed the passage to stand thirty years later in the sixth edition of the *Theory*, he never published this account.

We can however discover the main themes and the manner in which he tackled them from reports of the Glasgow lectures, based on students' notes, which have recently been printed.[9]

In these lectures, Smith took Hutcheson's scheme as his model, and at first sight seems to be offering an account of natural rights in the tradition of Grotius and Pufendorf. But he had assimilated the teaching of Hume on the gradual development of conventions concerning property, and of Montesquieu concerning the relations of law to the particular circumstances of society. He was well versed in the descriptions of the American Indians, and was sensitive to similarities between their style of life and that of the ancient Greeks, as suggested by Lafitau. All these influences blended to produce the philosophical history of legal institutions for which Kames and his salon were looking. One further influence can

---

[8] D. Stewart, 'Account of the Life and Writings of Adam Smith, LL.D.' (1793), *Collected Works* (10 vols., Edinburgh, 1854–60, reprinted Farnborough, 1971), x.12.

[9] Smith, *Lectures on Jurisprudence*.

perhaps be discerned, that of Machiavelli, whom Smith admired,[10] and of the writers on political theory in his tradition.

Machiavelli saw the welfare of the state as dependent on the readiness of her citizens to defend it personally by their own arms. When, however, well-disciplined armies of citizen–soldiers have secured military victory and established peace for their country, they have a tendency to allow their military prowess to degenerate into laziness. They use the wealth, which they derive from peace, to pay mercenaries to defend them instead of defending themselves, and they become corrupt as well as lazy. At this point they are forced to pull themselves together and start again. Machiavelli expressed the cycle of order and disorder like this:

> In their normal variations, countries generally go from order to disorder and then from disorder move back to order, because – since Nature does not allow worldly things to remain fixed – when they come to their utmost perfection and have no further possibility for rising, they must go down. Likewise, when they have gone down and through their defects have reached the lowest depths, they necessarily rise, since they cannot go lower. So always from good they go down to bad, and from bad rise up to good. Because ability brings forth quiet; quiet, laziness; laziness, disorder; disorder, ruin; and likewise from ruin comes order; from order, ability; from the last, glory and good fortune.[11]

Machiavelli had an English follower, James Harrington, who in 1656 published an idealised description of what England might become, called *Oceana*. Harrington viewed military service not so much as an expression of civic virtue, as Machiavelli had done, but as a function of feudal tenure and so based on the possession of property in land. The feudal vassal's service was at the disposal of his lord, but the freeholder's was available to defend the commonwealth.

Harrington cited Hobbes' remark that the law without a sword behind it was but paper, and added

> so he might have thought of this sword, that without an hand it is but cold iron. The hand which holdeth this sword is the militia of a nation...but an army is a beast that hath a great belly and must be fed; wherefore this will come unto

---

[10] In *Lectures on Rhetoric and Belles Lettres*, ed. J. M. Lothian (London, 1963), 110–11, he commends Machiavelli as the only modern historian 'who has contented himself with that which is the chief purpose of history, to relate events and connect them with their causes, without becoming a party on either side'.

[11] *History of Florence*, Book v, ch. 1, in *Chief Works*, translated by A. Gilbert (Durham, N.C., 1965), 1232.

what pastures you have and what pastures you have will come unto the balance of property, without which the public sword is but a name or a mere spitfrog.[12]

Harrington recognised property in land as the basis of political power and in his view changes in the form of government were dictated by changes in the control of land. Political institutions could then be seen to follow a cyclical pattern.

Ancient Rome was originally a commonwealth of freeholding citizen–soldiers, but the class of yeoman farmers was destroyed by the conquests of the Roman army and the growth of the great estates. The efforts of the Gracchi to stop the concentration of power in the hands of a few great land-owners were unsuccessful. The Caesars and their dependent armies then established an unstable monarchy in which land and power were shared between the Emperor and the Senate. To defend themselves, they eventually turned to the Goths as mercenaries, and the Goths finally took over the Empire and set up the feudal system throughout Europe. This in turn became a 'wrestling match' between king and nobility. In England the Tudors freed the military tenants from the authority of their feudal lords, and the stage was set for the rise of a new land-owning class of citizen–soldiers.

Harrington thus made the principle that distribution of land determines political power 'a key to unlock the whole course of western history'.[13] It enabled him to portray it as a chain of causes and effects linking the golden age of ancient Rome with the ideal commonwealth that England might soon become, if it only kept the ownership of land sufficiently widely dispersed among its citizens.

What Smith no doubt found attractive in this line of thought, apart from its emphasis on the connection between changes in control of land and changes in form of government, was the neat cyclical pattern which it gave to the major periods of European history. It had a relentless 'philosophical' quality in showing how states got into a certain condition, but it did not make the result entirely inevitable. The citizens of a state could themselves determine their future, provided that they had the will.

Having defined jurisprudence at the beginning of his Lectures

[12] *The Political Works of James Harrington*, ed. J. G. A. Pocock (Cambridge, 1977), 165.
[13] J. G. A. Pocock, *The Ancient Constitution and the Feudal Law* (Cambridge, 1957), 144.

as 'the theory of the rules by which civil governments ought to be directed', Smith announces that 'the first and chief design of every system of government is to maintain justice', which he understands as 'to prevent the members of a society from incroaching on one another's property' (p. 5). Justice is defined in terms of rights. 'Justice is violated whenever one is deprived of what he had a right to and could justly demand from others, or rather, when we do him any injury or hurt without a cause' (p. 7). In treating the different rights which a man enjoys, Smith follows the scheme adopted by his teacher Francis Hutcheson, who divided rights into three classes: those a man has as an individual, those he has as a member of a family and those he has as a citizen of a state. The injury which he suffers, and consequently the right which he enjoys, depends on the quality in which he is considered. Smith stressed that when he speaks of rights he means only what he calls perfect or legal rights as opposed to imperfect or moral rights. He was critical of the natural lawyers for blurring this distinction. He was very conscious of the limitations of the legal process: the law cannot make men better men. In the last resort all it can do is to make them pay money, or put them in prison, if they infringe the legal rights of others. So a man has a legal right to his reputation, and when another defames him by calling him a rogue or a knave when he is not such, he can sue; but he has only an imperfect or moral right that others should praise him for his remarkable learning, if he deserves such praise.

So far there is nothing about Smith's scheme that an orthodox natural lawyer could not have accepted. It is when he deals with the most important of the rights which a man enjoys as a man, namely his estate, that he introduces a new note. Estate includes both rights to property and personal rights arising from contract or deliquency. To understand the foundation from which these rights arise, argues Smith, we must know what stage of development the society in question had reached. For the law relating to property rights varies considerably from one stage to another. He then introduces the four stages through which societies pass: 'first, the Age of Hunters; secondly, the Age of Shepherds; thirdly, the Age of Agriculture; and fourthly, the Age of Commerce' (p. 14).

Thereafter in the lectures the four-stage theory is related to the explanation of legal rights. It is prominent in the first section: man's rights as an individual; and in the third section: man's rights as a citizen of a state. It is not so evident in the second section: man's rights as a member of a family.

Smith never considers man in an isolated state. In the earliest type of society, that of hunters, a nation consists of a number of independent families, there is very little in the way of government or law, there is almost no private property, theft is unimportant. Matters which concern only the members of a family are dealt with within the family.

> Disputes betwixt others can in this state but rarely occur, but if they do, and are of such a nature as would be apt to disturb the community, the whole community then interferes to make up the difference; which is ordinarily all the length they go, never daring to inflict what is properly called punishment. The design of their intermeddling is to preserve the public quiet, and the safety of the individuals; they therefore endeavour to bring about a reconcilement betwixt the parties at variance (p. 201).

This is proved by the state of the American Indians.

It is at the second stage, that of shepherds, that government proper begins. This stage cannot co-exist with the first. 'The appropriation of flocks and herds renders subsistence by hunting very uncertain and precarious.' The people are more numerous than at the hunting stage, and live a nomadic life, following the best grazing. Animals are now regarded as the property of particular individuals. 'The distinctions of rich and poor then arise' (p. 202).

> When...some have great wealth and others nothing, it is necessary that the arm of authority should be continually stretched forth, and permanent laws or regulations made which may ascertain [i.e. secure] the property of the rich from the inroads of the poor...Laws and government may be considered in this and indeed in every case as a combination of the rich to oppress the poor, and preserve to themselves the inequality of the goods which would otherwise be soon destroyed by the attacks of the poor, who if not hindered by the government would soon reduce the others to an equality with themselves by open violence. The government and laws hinder the poor from ever acquiring the wealth by violence which they would otherwise exert on the rich; they tell them they must either continue poor or acquire wealth in the same manner as they have done. Settled laws, therefore, or agreements concerning property, will soon be made after the commencement of the age of shepherds (pp. 208-9).

The administration of these laws is left to the whole community in popular assembly.

At this stage offences against property become more serious than they were among a hunting society. In the last resort, the community would expel the offender. Smith likens society in the pastoral stage to a club. 'The members of any club have it in their power to turn out any member, and so also have the members of such a community'(p. 204).

> As every club or society has a title to say to the several members of it Either submit to the regulations we make or get you about your business, so the community may say to the individuals who are members of it, Either make your behaviour agreable to our laws and rules or depart from amongst us (p. 209).

Smith makes it clear that these laws are conventions, settled practices rather than the enactments of a legislature. 'The legislative is never met with amongst people in this state of society'; it is 'the product of more refind manners and improved government' (p. 205).

The popular assembly would be presided over by a rich man who had acquired flocks, and had emerged as chief. Those who had no flocks of their own would have to perform services for those who did, and so would become dependent on them. Eventually, the chief's authority, based on his wealth and the number of his dependents, would become hereditary. As examples of societies at this stage of development, Smith cites the more backward peoples at the time of the Trojan Wars, described by Homer, whom Smith treats almost as a writer on social anthropology; the German tribes, described in Tacitus' *Germania*, and the Jews in the patriarchal period, described in Genesis. He stresses that the biblical patriarchs owed their authority to their wealth in terms of flocks. As a modern example of a society still in the pastoral stage, he cites the Tartars on the steppes of central Asia, living in nomadic tribes under the rule of despotic chiefs.

At this stage, considers Smith, there is very little cause for private litigation among the members of the society, as opposed to the punishment of offences against the community. In his own day, the bulk of law-suits arose from three situations: disputes over wills, disputes about marriage settlements, and disputes about contracts. Both wills and marriage settlements were unknown in the pastoral age, and contracts were not much developed, so that there was little occasion for disputes giving rise to civil litigation.

Private property in land, the most important item of property, was recognised only in the third stage, that of agriculture, and even then not immediately. Originally land would be cultivated collectively, but later it was divided up for individual use. Smith argues that at first property in land only continued as long as the land was actually being cultivated, and did not persist once the crop was out of the ground. As evidence he cites the practice, among country folk in Scotland, of letting their cattle wander wherever they wanted, as soon as the crop was lifted. This was in fact contrary to the Winter Herding Act of 1686, which ordered farmers to keep their cattle herded in winter, as well as in summer, under penalty of half a merk for each beast found on a neighbour's land. The ordinary people ignored the statute, and its penalties, Smith said, for they were 'so wedded to the notion that property in land continues no longer than the crop is on the ground that there is no possibility of getting them to observe it' (p. 23).

At this stage property remains the basis of power, and there is still a division in society between those who own the means of subsistence and those who must somehow acquire it. The latter can only acquire it by becoming dependants of some chief or lord. Although there are fewer opportunities for robbery and rustling than in the pastoral stage, now, 'many ways are added in which property may be interrupted as the subjects of it are considerably extended' (p. 16).

It is now that regular courts are established and legislation begins. The possibility of advancement beyond this stage depends on the ability of the society to produce a surplus of produce beyond its own immediate needs and on the opportunity to export that surplus to other societies.

For a people who are 'settled in a country where they lived in pretty great ease and security and in a soil capable of yielding them good returns for cultivation, would not only improve the earth but also make considerable advances in the severall arts and sciences and manufactures, providing they had an opportunity of exporting their sumptuous [*sic*] produce and fruits of their labour' (p. 223). The Tartars and Arabs lacked these conditions and so did not advance; the Greeks on the other hand, possessed both and could enter the stage of commerce. A further extension and complication of laws is needed for this fourth stage.

So far as concerns forms of government, changes in the ownership of property and political changes go hand in hand. Smith envisages a kind of cyclical evolution of types of government, each of which 'seems to have a certain and fixed end which concludes it' (p. 238). In a neo-Machiavellian manner, he portrays the history of Europe as two revolutions of the cycle.

The tribal chiefs leave the country and migrate to cities, which become populous. Not being prepared to tolerate the power of a monarch, the chiefs demand a share in the government, which thereupon becomes aristocratic. As commerce grows, the aristocratic government in turn gives way to a more democratic form of government. These democracies tend either to become small defensive republics, large cities in the middle of small territories, such as the Greek city states (and later the medieval Italian city states); or else they become large conquering republics, like Rome or Carthage.

The defensive republics end by being defeated by the conquering republics. Their military strength is insufficient for their defence. For whereas among hunters and shepherds, and in the early agricultural community, all citizens are fighting men, this ceases to be so when citizens engage in arts, manufactures and handicrafts, since they cannot be spared for fighting without ruining production. The lesson of history is that whenever 'arts and commerce engage the citizens, either as artisans or as master trades men, the strength and force of the city must be very much diminished' (p. 232).

The large conquering states have a similar problem. As the standard of living rises, the rich will no longer serve in the army; military service is the province of the lower orders, and standing armies of professional soldiers are created, whose loyalty is to their own general rather than to the state. These generals then take over the state. Having become emperors, they assume control of the executive and most of the legislature. Once again, as manufactures, trade and attendant luxury occupy the people, the government has recourse to mercenaries to defend the Empire. The leaders of the mercenaries turn against their paymasters.

This is what happened at the end of the Roman Empire. The barbarian successors to the Roman Empire were only at the hunting or pastoral stage. When the Romans were no longer able to defend the province of Britain, they left the Britons to defend themselves against 'the Scots and Picts, two nations who as we see from the poems of Ossian were much in the same state as the Americans, tho they don't appear to have had the custom of roasting men alive' (p. 239).

The cycle of change then began again. The provincial land was divided among the chiefs of the successor states as their own (allodial) property. Jurisdiction was localised, government was democratic, there was little industry and commerce. The chiefs gave their surplus property to dependants, who came to owe them services and enjoy their protection and so the feudal system grew up.

Smith notes that changes in private law do not necessarily accompany political changes. The Roman Emperors, for example, had no interest in changing the private law affecting ordinary citizens. 'The private affairs of individuals continued to be decided in the same manner and in the same courts as before. The emperor had no interest he could obtain by altering those forms, and on the other hand the people would more readily submit to his authority when they were allowed to continue' (p. 237). Indeed, although some people near to the centre of government were massacred, 'those who lived at a distance from the court were under a mild government, and lived more peaceably and happily than they did under the Republick, as the governors were more frequently called to an account, and the people could always appeal' (p. 241).

In general, however, the principle of development is that 'the more improved any society is and the greater length the severall means of supporting the inhabitants are carried, the greater will be the number of their laws and regulations necessary to maintain justice, and prevent infringements of the right of property' (p. 16). Locke had expressed something of this idea (*Of Civil Government*, sec. 124), but Smith makes it the basis of his whole treatment of rights. Property means something quite different according to the state of progress a society has reached. It is no good talking in general terms about property; we have to know what kind of society we are discussing and what are the current ideas about private property.

Smith argued that a man could be said to have suffered an injury, only 'when an impartial spectator would be of opinion that he was injured, would join with him in his concern, and go along with him' if he defended his property against attack or tried to recover what had been wrongfully taken from him (p. 17). At times some nations will have reached one stage of development while their neighbours will be at a more primitive stage, and this will be reflected in popular attitudes. Homer attests that at the time of the Trojan War, piratical expeditions against wealthy neighbours were not considered dishonourable.

Odysseus, when asked whether he was a merchant or a pirate, says he was a pirate:

> This was a much more honourable character than that of a merchant, which was allways looked on with great contempt by them. A pirate is a military man who acquires his livelyhood by warlike exploits, whereas a merchant is a peaceable one who has no occasion for military skill and would not be much esteemed in a nation consisting of warriors chiefly (p. 224).

The significance of Smith's evolutionary approach for jurisprudence is that it enabled him to explain the basis of legal institutions in a different way from that of the writers in the natural law tradition. They had stressed the will of the individuals involved in a transaction, and set it against the good of the community as a whole.

A vital institution in private law is contract, and Smith differed from Grotius and Pufendorf in his explanation of the nature of contractual obligation. The traditional explanation was that what made a contract binding was the promisor's declaration of his will which bound him to keep his word (*De iure belli*, II.11; *De iure naturae*, III.5). Smith argued that the binding force derived from the expectation which the promisor's declaration created in the promisee.[14] An impartial spectator would not always consider that every declaration of intent should be relied on by the promisee.

Thus primitive societies make light of breaches of contract and do not always hold contracts binding. He quotes Nicolaos of Damascus to the effect that among Eastern nations 'no contract was binding, not even that of restoring a depositum, that in which the obligation seems to be strongest as the injury in the breach of it is most glaring' (p. 88). It is only with the advance of commerce

---

[14] Hints of this approach in Hutcheson, *System*, II.1ff; Hume, *Treatise*, III.2.5; Kames, *Essays on the Principles of Morality and Natural Religion* (Edinburgh, 1751), 1.2.7.

that contracts become frequent. Only then is there a need for credit to be given and only then does an informal promise reasonably create in the promisee a ground of expectation, which would be disappointed if the promise were not fulfilled. The extent of the obligation is measured by the disappointment the breach of it would occasion. Smith enumerates the causes of the late introduction of enforceable agreements in most legal systems as first, 'the smallness of the injury' caused by breach of contract as compared with infringement of property; secondly, 'the uncertainty of language' making it hard to decide if a man was binding himself or merely signifying his intention; thirdly, 'the difficulty and inconvenience of obtaining a trial of any crime' when the whole body of people have to be assembled to judge it. Breaches of contract cause little civil disturbance, so that it is some time before they are distinguished from injuries which do, such as murder, robbery and the like; and fourthly, 'the small value of the things which contract could include in the early times' (p. 94).

Related to contract is the problem which arises when a sum of money is borrowed, and before the time of repayment, the money is called in and a new coinage is introduced, with a reduced value at the old denominations. 'Here the civil law of all countries and naturall justice and equity are quite contrary. Justice and equity plainly require that one should restore the same value as he received without regard to the nominal value of money...But the civil government in all countries have constituted the exact contrary of this.' The reason is that the government only reduces the value of money when it has difficulty in raising money. By debasing the coinage they can pay their own expenses and loans with perhaps half the real value. 'But lest the imposition should be too soon felt by the creditors of the government, they ordered that all debts should in like manner be paid by the new coin. This expedient concealed the fraud' (pp. 100–1).

With regard to property, most systems recognise prescription as a method of acquiring ownership of a thing by the possession of it for a considerable period. The traditional view was that it was based on the presumed will of the former owner to abandon it, if he allowed another to possess for so long (*De iure belli*, II.4). But, says Smith, 'no one would willingly give up a right to a considerable estate' (p. 36). The foundation of prescriptive right is surely 'the attachment the possessor may be supposed to have formed to what he has long possessed; and the detachment of the former possessor's affection from what had for a long time been altogether out of his power'.[15] The impartial spectator is invoked to decide at what point the long possessor 'has a just expectation that he may use what has been thus possessed, and...the former proprietor has so far lost all right to it, has no expectation of using it, as that it would appear injurious in him to deprive the present possessor' (p. 32).

Again, when dealing with acquisition of property by succession on death, Smith differs from Grotius and Pufendorf. They explain intestate succession as based on the supposed will of the deceased (*De iure belli*, II.7.3; *De iure naturae*, IV.11.1). The deceased normally expresses his intentions in his will, but if he fails to make a will, the law distributes his estate as he is presumed to have intended. This kind of explanation, argues Smith, is quite unhistorical because it implies that testamentary succession preceded intestate succession. In all societies, ancient and modern, the reverse is the case. The right to dispose of one's property after death by will 'is one of the greatest extensions of property we can conceive, and consequently would not be early introduced into society' (p. 38). In the age of hunters, there was no succession at all, a man's personal belongings, his weapons, being buried with him. In later stages of society, property was regarded as family property 'which as it was maintained and procured by the labour of the whole family, was also the common support of the whole' (p. 39). The head of the family alone could alienate family property in his lifetime, but not at his death. Roman law shows that originally all the descendants came in for an equal share of their father's goods, not because it was his will that they should do so but because they were continuing their possession of what they themselves had helped to procure and maintain.

Smith observes that the rules of intestate succession to moveables were essentially governed by the same principles in ancient Rome and modern Europe. The only significant difference was in the share of the widow in her husband's estate – which was slight in

[15] cf. Kames, *Essays on several subjects in Law* (Edinburgh, 1732), No. IV.

Rome compared with modern societies. The explanation for this difference is to be found in the distinction between Roman marriage which was freely dissoluble and Christian marriage which was not (p. 47).

Again when dealing with rights arising from delinquency, Smith's historical approach leads him to a different explanation from that of the natural law writers. They had argued that the basis of punishment for crime was consideration of the public good (*De iure belli*, II.20.7; *De iure naturae*, VIII.3.9). The real source, said Smith, must be the resentment of the injured party, and so the measure of punishment is the point at which the view of the impartial spectator concurs with that of the victim of the crime in the manner of his revenge (p. 104).

In early societies it was left to the victim to get his own satisfaction for crimes.

> In the description of the shield of Achilles, in one of the compartments the story represented is the friends of a slain man receiving presents from the slayer. The government did not then intermeddle in those affairs; and we find that the stranger who comes on board the ship of Telemachus tells us he fled from the friends of a man whom he had slain, and not from the officers of justice (p. 108).

If the injury is so great that the spectator can go along with the injured person in revenging himself by the death of the offender, that is the proper punishment, which is to be exacted by the victim or the magistrate acting the character of the impartial spectator. If the impartial spectator will only go along with a pecuniary penalty, then that is the punishment which ought to be inflicted.

To prove his point, that the measure of punishment is what the impartial spectator at the relevant time and place will go along with, Smith cites a contemporary example. The British people conceived the 'whimsical' notion that its prosperity depended on the woollen goods trade and therefore made the exportation of wool a felony punishable by death. But since in natural equity this exportation was no crime at all, it was found impossible to get informers or juries who would convict. So the punishment had to be reduced to what was acceptable (pp. 104–5).

When tracing the development of particular legal institutions in detail, Smith was largely restricted to two systems for his illustrations, Roman law and English law. The Roman legal sources documented the development of the system for over a thousand years of antiquity – from the Twelve Tables in the fifth century B.C. to the legislation of the sixth century A.D. – to say nothing of developments after the medieval revival of legal studies. Furthermore, non-legal Latin literature provided the social background against which the law evolved. Only English law provided a similarly detailed set of sources for tracing its development. It had borrowed less from Roman law than any other system, and for that reason Smith felt it was closer to nature. It is 'more deserving of the attention of a speculative man than any other, as being more formed on the naturall sentiments of mankind' (p. 98). The Scots lawyers of Kames' circle, with their interest in unification of law, were more conscious than their contemporaries in England of legal systems other than their own. Smith showed himself at home in both Roman law and English law as well as Scots law, and could draw parallels from their respective histories.

When dealing with man's rights as a member of a family, he traces the development of the marriage laws of Rome. In the earliest times the wife was absolutely in the power of her husband. At this period, Smith explains, the fortune a woman could bring to her husband on marriage was very small and insufficient to entitle her to bargain with him; her only option was to submit to his power. However, as the wealth of the community increased, rich heiresses became not uncommon and a new kind of marriage was introduced in their favour. In the dowry settlement the terms on which the husband was to enjoy the wife's property were agreed and she no longer entered his power. This new sort of marriage, 'tho it had none of the old solemnities, was found by the lawyers to save the lady's honour and legitimate the children' (p. 144). It was created by consent and could be dissolved by the will of either party. Since it was found to be much more convenient and adapted to the licentiousness of the times, the old forms were abandoned. Smith enjoyed showing that the newer free marriage was itself 'productive of the worst consequences. It tended plainly to corrupt the moralls of the women. The wives often passed thro' 4 or 5 different husbands, which tended to give them but very loose notions of chastity and good behaviour' (p. 145).

After the fall of the Roman Empire, however, the barbarian

successor societies were in an earlier stage of development in which the wife was still under the subjection of her husband, and later, as a result of the influence of the Christian clergy, marriage came to be almost indissoluble. Smith takes the opportunity in this context to make some curious comments on the change which he considers this indissolubility of marriage produced in the character of 'the passion of love'.

> This passion was formerly esteemed to be a very silly and ridiculous one... There is no poem of a serious nature grounded on that subject either amongst the Greeks or Romans. There is no ancient tragedy, except Phaedra, the plot of which turns on a love story, tho there are many on all other passions, as anger, hatred, revenge, ambition etc.

The story of Dido in the *Aeneid* is in no sense a love story, nor is the *Iliad*.

> The cause of the Trojan War was the rape of Helen, etc., but what sort of a love story is it? Why, the Greek chiefs combine to bring back Helen to her husband; but he never expresses the least indignation against her for her infidelity. It is all against Paris, who carried away his wife along with his goods...
> The reason why this passion made so little figure then in comparison of what it now does is plainly this. The passion itself is... of nature rather ludicrous; the frequency and easiness of divorce made the gratification of it of no great moment... The choice of the person was of no very great importance, as the union might be dissolved at any time. This was the case both amongst the Greeks and Romans. But when marriage became indissoluble, the matter was greatly altered. The choice of the object of this passion, which is commonly the forerunner of marriage, became a matter of the greatest importance. The union was perpetual and consequently the choice of the person was a matter which would have a great influence on the future happiness of the parties. From that time therefore we find that love makes the subject of all our tragedies and romances (pp. 149-50).

(Smith himself was a life-long bachelor.)

There is a robust commonsense quality about his explanations. He preferred down-to-earth explanations to subtle ones. The rule found in many systems, that a husband can divorce his wife for her adultery but she has no corresponding right, was not designed, as was usually claimed, to prevent spurious offspring being imposed on the husband. 'The real reason is that it is men who make the laws with respect to this; they generally will be inclined to curb the women as much as possible and give themselves the more indulgence' (p. 147).

Smith came to his theory of legal evolution as a moral philosopher. To test his explanations of moral duties, he felt the need for an empirical base. At each point he measures his propositions against common experience, which he calls nature. This is not an *a priori* concept, based on armchair deductions from reason. What is natural for Smith is what normally happens or what would happen but for the presence of some distinctively human factor. Instinctive or spontaneous behaviour is natural, but an act may also become natural as a result of habit, custom and education. What is natural for a society is decided by the stage of development which that society has reached.

Smith could still regard himself as, in a sense, building on the natural law tradition because, unlike Hume, he was a deist. His deism enabled him to see the scheme by which societies developed from stage to stage as part of the plan of an all-wise Author of Nature, whose invisible hand had shaped the design. This belief encouraged him to seek the systematic aspects of societal progress, and when he did discover them, they in turn confirmed him in his belief in God. God lays down the general course that a society will naturally take, but human action can prevent it from taking that course. As Professor T. D. Campbell puts it,

> His argument from design...only commits him to the view that, when human will does not change the spontaneous behaviour of men in society, the usual consequences of such behaviour are beneficial to most members of that society. This leaves him scope for encouraging spontaneous behaviour and even suggesting that men improve on the economy of nature by remedying some of the defects of a system that is on the whole good, but may have incongruous and unhappy consequences on occasion.[16]

Social institutions grow up and change in response to a wide variety of factors although the economic factor is the most decisive. The process is not without resistance; custom and habit and the vested interests of declining groups can maintain institutions long after the causes which produced them have ceased to operate.

This enables Smith to hold both that social and legal institutions are the natural result of man's interaction with his environment, and that particular institutions at a particular time are a hindrance to natural liberty. Natural liberty is not an absence of institutional restraints; rather it presupposes the operation of those institutions

[16] *Adam Smith's Science of Morals* (London, 1971), 62.

which allow spontaneous human behaviour to show itself in a way appropriate to each stage of societal development. Discussing certain banking laws in *The Wealth of Nations*, he says, 'Such regulations may, no doubt, be considered as in some respect a violation of natural liberty. But those exertions of the natural liberty of a few individuals, which might endanger the security of the whole society, are, and ought to be, restrained by the laws of all governments; of the most free, as well as the most despotical' (p. 324). Natural liberty implies, then, a set of laws and institutions designed to make the self-interested actions of individual men work to the advantage of all. The appropriate analogy for such laws is no longer mathematics, as it was for the rationalist natural law theorists. It is rather the rules of grammar, established by a slow process of social consensus, and subject to human alteration (*Theory of Moral Sentiments*, p. 175).

JOHN MILLAR

Adam Smith never published the lectures on jurisprudence and was not professionally a lawyer. His ideas were developed, popularised and disseminated by his pupil, John Millar, who became Professor of Civil Law at Glasgow at the age of twenty-six. Millar's main works were *Observations concerning the Distinction of Ranks in Society*, published in 1771, and *An Historical view of English Government, from the Settlement of the Saxons in Britain to the Accession of the House of Stewart* (1787).[17]

Millar saw himself as continuing the movement of thought about law, begun by Montesquieu and continued by Kames and Smith.

The attempts to delineate systems of jurisprudence...opened at length a new source of speculation, by suggesting an inquiry into the circumstances which have occasioned various and opposite imperfections in the law of different countries, and which have prevented the practical systems, in any, from attaining that improvement which we find no difficulty in conceiving. In the prosecution of this inquiry, more especially by President Montesquieu, by Lord Kames and by Dr

---

[17] The earlier work appeared in 1779 in a revised form as *The Origin of the Distinction of Ranks* with the subtitle *An Inquiry into the Circumstances which give rise to Influence and Authority in the different Members of Society*. W. C. Lehmann, *John Millar of Glasgow, 1735–1801* (Cambridge, 1960), reprints *The Origin of Ranks* in full and selections from *An Historical View*; Meek, *Social Science*, 160–76.

Smith, the attention of speculative lawyers has been directed to examine the first formation and subsequent advancement of civil society; the rise, the gradual development and cultivation of arts and sciences; the acquisition and extension of property in all its modifications, and the combined influence of these and other political causes, upon the manners and customs, the institutions and the laws of any people (Lehmann, 347).[18]

Millar recognised that the 'inquiry' to which he referred had moved the focus of legal thought from the natural lawyer's pre-occupation with what ought to be the law to a concern with what laws men in different societies actually observe. This change of emphasis was part of a general interest, particularly prevalent in Scotland, in establishing the facts of society, which was symbolised in the twenty-one volumes of the *Statistical Account of Scotland*,[19] a descriptive account of the state of the whole country, parish by parish.

Millar sought a philosophy of history which could penetrate 'beneath that common surface of events which occupies the details of the vulgar historian',[20] and set out its guiding principles with great lucidity in the introduction to *The Origin of Ranks*: 'In searching for the causes of those peculiar systems of law and government which have appeared in the world, we must undoubtedly resort, first of all, to the differences of situation, which have suggested different views and motives of action to the inhabitants of particular countries'; the kind of soil, climate, number of the population, their proficiency in arts, and so on. The variety of these particulars 'must have a prodigious influence upon the great body of a people; as by giving a peculiar direction to their inclinations and pursuits, it must be productive of correspondent habits, dispositions and ways of thinking'.

He then expresses his unequivocal belief in the progress of society. Despite the barbarism of some societies, there is 'in man a disposition and capacity for improving his condition, by the

---

[18] cf. 'The great Montesquieu pointed out the road. He was the Lord Bacon in this branch of study; Dr. Smith is the Newton' (in Lehmann, 363). In regard to the relationship between law and the facts of economic and social life, Millar refers, in addition to Adam Smith, to Sir Thomas Smith's *Commonwealth of England* (1565), on which see P. Stein, 'Sir Thomas Smith, Renaissance Civilian', in *Essays in Honour of B. Beinart*, III, *Acta Juridica* (1978), 79–89; and to James Harrington's *Oceana* (ante, p. 31).

[19] Ed. Sir John Sinclair (Edinburgh, 1791–9).

[20] *Historical View* (London, 1812), IV.101.

exertion of which, he is carried on from one degree of advancement to another; and the similarity of his wants, as well as of the faculties by which those wants are supplied, has every where produced a remarkable uniformity in the several steps of his progression'.

As men move from the stages of hunting to taming and rearing cattle, and then to cultivating the ground,

> their prospects are gradually enlarged, their appetites and desires are more and more awakened and called forth in the pursuit of the several conveniences of life; and the various branches of manufacture, together with commerce, its inseparable attendant, and with science and literature, the natural offspring of ease and affluence, are introduced, and brought to maturity...property, the great source of distinction among individuals, is established; and the various rights of mankind, arising from their multiplied connections, are recognised and protected: the laws of a country are thereby rendered numerous; and a more complex form of government becomes necessary, for distributing justice, and for preventing the disorders which proceed from the jarring interests and passions of a large and opulent community...There is thus, in human society, a natural progress from ignorance to knowledge, and from rude to civilized manners, the several stages of which are usually accompanied with peculiar laws and customs (Lehmann, 175–6).

Millar insisted on the dependence of legal progress on economic and social progress, and urged the need for accurate historical investigation of legal experience. 'Of all the sciences, law seems to be that which depends most upon experience and in which mere speculative reasoning is of the least consequence.' The value of Roman law is that it rests upon 'the accumulated experience and observation of ages and of the most extensive empire that ever existed in a civilized form' (Lehmann, 113).

Millar's formulation of the evolutionary idea seems more full-blooded than that of his contemporaries. He was not a complete determinist. In theory he recognised that 'various accidental causes, indeed, have contributed to accelerate, or to retard' the advancement of law. He accepted that people may become 'so habituated to the peculiar manners' of a particular age 'as to retain a strong tincture of those peculiarities, through every subsequent revolution' (Lehmann, 176–7). Yet in practice he was unwilling to allow much effect to accidental causes. Discussing the revival of Roman law in the twelfth century, he was sceptical about the opinion that it was due to the accidental discovery of a manuscript of Justinian's *Digest* at Amalfi. 'We may be allowed to entertain some doubt, whether an event of that magnitude could have proceeded from a circumstance so frivolous.'[21]

Certainly to his contemporaries, Millar appeared to be more thorough-going a determinist than other writers. Francis Jeffery, his pupil and admirer, considered that

it was the leading principle... of all his speculations on law, morality, government, language, the arts, sciences and manners – that there is nothing produced by arbitrary or accidental causes; that no change, institution, custom or occurrence could be ascribed to the character or exertions of an individual, to the temperament or disposition of a nation, to occasional policy, or peculiar wisdom or folly; everything, on the contrary, he held arose spontaneously from the situation of the society, and was suggested or imposed irresistibly by the opportunities or necessities of their condition.[22]

Fraser Tytler, Lord Woodhouselee, accused Millar of allowing no influence to accidental circumstances or individual actions, and argued that he held 'that all arises necessarily, by a uniform and natural process, which can neither be effectually resisted, nor prematurely accelerated'.[23]

In *The Origin of Ranks* Millar has much of interest to say on the development of family institutions, of the changes in the authority of the father over his children and the position of the wife as society passed through the various stages from hunting to commerce. Discussing 'the rank and condition of women', he points out that in some countries, before marriage as an institution is established, the mother is head of the family and 'will often be raised to a degree of rank and dignity to which from her sex, she would not otherwise be entitled' (Lehmann, 199); and he gives several examples of matriarchal societies. When marriage is first established, the condition of wives is almost servile, but it improves as society develops.

This progress, however, is slow and gradual; at the same time that, from the uniformity of the human constitution, it is accompanied with similar appearances in different parts of the world. When agriculture has created abundance of provisions, people extend their views to other circumstances of smaller importance... manufactures, together with commerce, are at length introduced into a country. These improvements are the source of very important changes in the state of society, and particularly in relation to the women. The advancement of people in manufactures and commerce has a natural tendency to remove those

[21] *ibid.*, II.321.   [22] *Edinburgh Review*, 3 (1803), 157.
[23] Tytler, *Memoirs of Kames*, I.280 n.

circumstances which prevented the free intercourse of the sexes, and contributed to heighten and inflame their passions... The men and women of different families are permitted to converse with more ease and freedom (Lehmann, 218-19).

As the wealth of a society increases, this process is extended, but there is a limit to the development. Millar concludes with a warning:

> Thus we may observe, that in refined and polished nations there is the same free communication between the sexes as in the ages of rudeness and barbarism. In the latter, women enjoy the most unbounded liberty, because it is thought of no consequence what use they shall make of it. In the former, they are entitled to the same freedom, upon account of those agreeable qualities which they possess, and the rank and dignity which they hold as members of society. It would seem, however, that there are certain limits beyond which it is impossible to push the real improvements arising from wealth and opulence. In a simple age, the free intercourse of the sexes is attended with no bad consequences; but in opulent and luxurious nations, it gives rise to licentious and dissolute manners, inconsistent with good order, and with the general interest of society. [Thus] the natural tendency... of great luxury and dissipation is to diminish the rank and dignity of the women (Lehmann, 225).

Millar did not give much attention to the evolution of particular legal doctrines. He presented his readers with broad views of the parallel and interconnected changes in law and society. His importance in the history of legal evolution is as a publicist. As Francis Jeffrey put it, he taught that we should not gaze 'with stupid amazement on the singular and diversified appearances of human institutions', but rather 'consider them as necessary links in the great chain which connects civilized with barbarous society'.[24]

---

[24] *Edinburgh Review*, 3 (1803), 157.

3

The German historical school of law

The growth of evolutionary theories of law in Germany has to be seen against the background of the prevailing type of natural law theory, which dominated legal thinking there in the late eighteenth century. Its two main exponents were Christian Thomasius (1655–1728) and Christian Wolff (1679–1754).[1]

Grotius and Pufendorf, in differing degrees, had held that natural law could be proved either *a posteriori*, by showing that certain principles had been accepted as law by different societies in the past, or *a priori*, by deducing it logically from the rational and social nature of man. Thomasius and Wolff scrapped the *a posteriori* method completely in favour of the *a priori* method. Thomasius held that natural law was the law of reason and rested entirely on deductions from common sense (*sensus communis*). Everyone, he believed, could feel in himself what was necessary for an understanding of the moral nature of man. The product of such rationalist speculation was not, however, in Thomasius' view, strictly law. For, like the Scottish thinkers, Thomasius distinguished sharply between morality and law. Law has a compulsory character; it is backed by the power of the state. It follows that law, strictly conceived, must be the command of the ruler, as it was for Hobbes, for only such commands as are backed by the ruler's power obligate the subjects in a coercive way. Natural law, therefore, becomes merely series of pieces of advice (*consilia*) to the legislator.[2] The enlightened ruler would, of course, welcome and

---

[1] F. Wieacker, *Privatrechtsgeschichte der Neuzeit*, 2nd edn (Göttingen, 1967), 314–21; for Thomasius, E. Wolf, *Grosse Rechtsdenker der Deutschen Geistesgeschichte*, 4th edn (Tübingen, 1963), 371–423.
[2] 'The wise man conceives God as a teacher of natural law rather than as a legislator', *Fundamenta iuris naturae* (1705), 1.5.40.

adopt the dictates of natural law and ensure that they became law in the positive sense, but ultimately what made a rule law was not that it was derived from reason but that it was the act of the ruler.

Whereas Thomasius came to law from theology, Wolff approached it from mathematics. He worked out a system of social and political thought marked by clarity and logical precision, in which the duties of the individual were set out in great detail. His main work, *Ius naturae methodo scientifica pertractum*, appeared in eight volumes (1740–8). It considerably softened the sharp distinction, drawn by Thomasius, between law and morals, and put forward an elaborate system of moral duties owed by everyone in society. 'No law exists without a moral obligation which precedes it, in which it is rooted, and from which it flows' (1.1.26). At the same time Wolff accepted the distinction between law accompanied by the right to coerce, which was more perfect, and that not so provided, which was less perfect, and he stressed the 'permissive' parts of natural law, which could be defined and redefined by the ruler.

The school of thought created by Thomasius and Wolff cut itself off from the study of actual legal systems. With characteristic eighteenth-century optimism, their followers believed that reason alone could show men the right way to behave in most situations of daily life. The elegant systems, so precisely expounded by them, were an obvious attraction to the enlightened rulers of the day. Once right conduct had been identified, they wanted to make it a matter of legal and not merely of moral obligation.

A whole series of codifications owed their origin to these rational systems of natural law: that of Bavaria in 1756, that of Prussia, begun by Frederick the Great and eventually promulgated in 1794, and that of Austria in 1811. The famous Prussian *Allgemeines Landrecht* is typical in its all-embracing scope. It contains sixteen thousand provisions, as compared with fewer than two and a half thousand in the *Code Napoléon* of 1804 or the *Bürgerliches Gesetzbuch* of 1896. They prescribe with mathematical precision what is right and what is wrong, and cover many matters which would be regarded today as quite inappropriate for legal regulation. Thus there is a detailed statement of the circumstances in which a wife is excused from her obligation to accord her husband his marital rights, for example, when she is breast-feeding a child (II.1.4, paras. 178–80).

The reaction against this rationalist form of natural law started significantly at Göttingen, the university of the Kingdom of Hanover, which was linked with Britain by a personal union. Göttingen was more open to foreign ideas than other German universities, and especially to down to earth breaths of empirical British air.

Johann Stephan Pütter, a professor of public law at Göttingen, thus described the effects of the trendy methods of legal thought which then prevailed:

> Young people especially were led to believe they knew a great deal, while in reality they knew nothing...And what was worse, people began so to underrate and neglect languages, philology, antiquities, history, observation, experience, positive laws and all the sources of knowledge to which access is more laborious and difficult than a definition and demonstration, brought out merely by reflection or cogitation, that Germany then ran great risk, of falling back into an actual state of barbarism if this taste had continued.[3]

There were, of course, historical studies, particularly of Roman law, but their contribution to a proper understanding of legal institutions was obscured by their emphasis on antiquarianism and their acceptance of Roman law as a finished product. Historical data were subordinated to the need to justify a particular interpretation of the Roman texts, which was required for contemporary practice.

The leading writer who represents this tendency was Johann Gottfried Heineccius, whose *Antiquitatum Romanarum Syntagma* ran into twenty editions in the century after its publication in 1719. It was much used as a reference book for the social background of Roman law by Adam Smith. Heineccius had a comprehensive knowledge of antiquity, and brought together a mass of curious detail on every topic. His aim was to illustrate, with as rich an accumulation of examples as possible, the various institutions of Roman law according to the order of Justinian's *Institutes*. But this detail was not harnessed to show how the institutions had developed. This was 'elegant jurisprudence', the data of antiquity being merely a decorative ornament to the needs of contemporary law.

---

[3] *Civilistisches Magazin*, 2.55, translated by James Reddie, *Inquiries elementary and historical in the Science of Law* (London, 1840), 41–2.

HUGO

The man who broke away from this kind of legal history, and at the same time resisted the excesses of rationalism, was Gustav Hugo (1764–1844),[4] another professor at Göttingen. Historical studies were more part of the atmosphere of that university than elsewhere and the kind of history taught was empirical and pragmatic. Hugo was the founder of the modern approach to the history of Roman law, which is based on the belief that a proper understanding of the texts which Justinian transmitted to us can only be achieved by studying the development of the law contained in those texts during the various periods through which Roman law had passed. Today we take this for granted, but in the late eighteenth century the law of Justinian's *Corpus Iuris* was regarded as *ratio scripta*, the embodiment of reason in writing.

For inspiration Hugo turned not to a German scholar but to an Englishman, Edward Gibbon.

The early volumes of Gibbon's *Decline and Fall of the Roman Empire* were published in 1776, the same year as the publication of Adam Smith's *Wealth of Nations*, and the later volumes in 1788. Gibbon had read, and been influenced by, several of the writers drawn on by Smith, especially Hume and Montesquieu, and had a high regard for the Scottish historical school. In the last volume, he writes: 'On this interesting subject, the progress of society in Europe, a strong ray of philosophic light has broke from Scotland in our own times; and it is with private, as well as public regard, that I repeat the names of Hume, Robertson and Adam Smith.'[5] Although most of the *Decline and Fall* was concerned with matters other than law, there was one chapter which was destined to have considerable influence on historical jurisprudence, the famous forty-fourth chapter on the development of Roman law from the early monarchy in the sixth century B.C. to the time of Justinian in the sixth century A.D.

What Gibbon did was to combine the ideas of conjectural or

---

[4] Wieacker, *Privatrechtsgeschichte*, 377–81; G. Marini, *L'opera di Gustav Hugo nella crisi del giusnaturalismo tedesco* (Milan, 1965).

[5] Ch. 61, n. 72; cf. Adam Smith's letter of congratulation to Gibbon, *The Correspondence of Adam Smith*, ed. E. C. Mossner and I. S. Ross (Oxford, 1977), No. 283.

philosophical historians with the attention to detail characteristic of the antiquarians such as Heineccius. Professor Momigliano puts it like this:

> Gibbon broke new ground not by his ideas on the decline of Rome, but by offering the treasures of erudition to the contemplation of the philosophic historian. By doing so, he unexpectedly reconciled two methods of writing history, which so far had seemed to be inevitably opposed. First of all, he presented the theories of the philosophic historians in a much more persuasive way. Secondly he showed that erudition did not necessarily imply lack of elegance and reflection... Something new came out of his combination. Philosophic history ceased to be approximate and arbitrary and was submitted to the traditional rules of historical criticism.[6]

The forty-fourth chapter[7] exemplifies this judgement. The subject of Roman law clearly engaged the author. 'The laws of a nation form the most instructive portion of its history; and although I have devoted myself to write the annals of a declining monarchy, I shall embrace the occasion to breathe the pure and invigorating air of the republic' (pp. 3–4).

The thrust of the chapter is the power of Roman law to adapt itself to changes in Roman society. Gibbon brings out the strictness and the symbolic character of the early legal forms. 'The jurisprudence of the first Romans exhibited the scenes of a pantomime' (p. 21). This early formalism was, however, overcome by the Roman jurists. Gibbon recognised that the history of Roman law was the story of the work of the jurists, who normally held no official position in the administration of justice, but made it their profession to become experts in the intricacies of the Roman law, and to ensure that it moved with the times. 'A more liberal art was cultivated by the sages of Rome, who in a stricter sense may be considered as the authors of the civil law.' Their 'noble task' was 'to define the ambiguities, to circumscribe the latitude, to apply the principles, to extend the consequences, to reconcile the real or apparent contradictions', so that 'however strange or intricate the means, it was the aim of artificial jurisprudence to restore the simple dictates of nature and reason, and the skill of private citizens was usefully employed to undermine the public institutions of their country' (p. 23).

'The revolution of almost one thousand years from the twelve

[6] *Studies in Historiography* (London, 1966), 51.
[7] I have used the 1811 edition, vol. VIII.

tables to the reign of Justinian, may be divided into three periods, almost equal in duration, and distinguished from each other by the mode of instruction and the character' of the jurists. The most important period was the middle period (now known as the classical period, the first two centuries of the Christian era).

Gibbon saw that, although the evidence for the controversies and arguments of the classical jurists had to a great extent been lost, this must have been a period of fierce discussion. Even the jurists were human beings, and in this regard he stressed the interest of the two schools of jurists, the Proculians and the Sabinians. 'Positive institutions are often the result of custom and prejudice; laws and language are ambiguous and arbitrary; where reason is incapable of pronouncing, the love of argument is inflamed by the envy of rivals, the vanity of masters, the blind attachment of their disciples' (p. 30).

Hugo translated the forty-fourth chapter into German. In presenting it to the public, he criticised the prevailing antiquarianism in legal history, and asserted that Montesquieu had shown how historical study of law should be carried out and that Gibbon had followed that way.[8]

In his later work Hugo attacked the prevailing vogue for statute law and codification which purported to make the function of the judge purely mechanical. In 1812, in an essay with the revealing title, 'Statutes are not the only sources of juristic truth',[9] he systematically rejected these ideas, showing how inadequate statute law was without the creative activity of judge and jurist.

SAVIGNY

The lead given by Hugo was developed by Friedrich Karl von Savigny (1779–1861),[10] who is usually considered the real founder

---

[8] Hugo, *Beyträge zur civilistischen Bücherkenntniss*, 1 (1828), 131.
[9] 'Die Gesetze sind nicht die einzige Quelle der juristischen Wahrheiten', *Civilistisches Magazin*, 4.89–134.
[10] Wieacker, *Privatrechtsgeschichte*, 381–99; Wieacker, *Gründer und Bewahrer* (Göttingen, 1959), 107–43; Wolf, *Grosse Rechtsdenker*, 467–542; F. Engel-Janosi, 'The intellectual background of Savigny', *Seminar* (1947), 39–59; 'Memoir of F. C. von Savigny', appendix v to Savigny, *A Treatise on the Conflict of Laws*, translated by W. Guthrie, 2nd edn (Edinburgh, 1880).

of the German historical school. He was a member of a noble family and at the time it was unusual for an aristocrat to follow an academic career. His writing always bore the confident, authoritative stamp of one who is secure in his social status. Hugo had been attracted by Montesquieu's pragmatic approach, but Savigny took up certain ideas adumbrated by Montesquieu, and developed them in a romantic, almost mystical way, which was foreign to Hugo. Montesquieu had argued that for a rule to be good law, it had to conform not to an abstract reason, but to the spirit of the society to which it was to be applied, and the spirit of a society was distilled from a variety of ingredients, climate, religion, social custom and so on. Savigny added a further ingredient to the mixture and he derived it largely from the Irishman, Edmund Burke, and his fellow countryman, Johann Gottfried Herder.

Burke's work was characterised by a distaste for logical speculation from abstract principles. Real life, he argued, was too complicated to apply to it, say, the principles of individual liberty, without careful regard for the consequences. He insisted on the application of moral principles in political life, but held that moral principles must be adjusted to the feelings and emotions of the people, and to their conflicting interests. Statesmen must take account of the emotional responses which the social order evokes in a society. Burke appreciated the irrational, intangible elements in the social order and stressed the need for balancing political principles, such as freedom or order, against these characteristics, in order to achieve a consensus view. His aim was, of course, to prevent the radical changes which the ideals of the French Revolution seemed to demand. He was too subtle to oppose all change; what he sought was change which was appropriate to the body politic.

Burke made full use of the metaphor of organic growth when dealing with the British constitution. When it was in its formative period, its growth was more visible than when it had attained the stage of maturity, as he claimed it had done since the Revolution of 1688.

To his continental readers, who were less concerned with the practical implications of his politics than his English readers, Burke conveyed a general sense of historical continuity and a particular vision of society. People will not look forward to posterity who never look backward to their ancestors. Society is

a partnership in all science; a partnership in all art; a partnership in every virtue and in all perfection. As the ends of such a partnership cannot be obtained in many generations, it becomes a partnership not only between those who are living, but between those who are living, those who are dead and those who are to be born. Each contract of each particular state is but a clause in the great primeval contract of eternal society.[11]

J. G. Herder also stressed the importance of tradition but for him what was important was not a political but a cultural tradition. Germany in his day was a collection of small principalities, none of which offered any scope for shared political activity. His central idea lies in the

assertion that the proper foundation for a sense of collective political identity is not the acceptance of a common sovereign power, but the sharing of a common culture. For the former is imposed from outside, whilst the latter is the expression of an inner consciousness, in terms of which each individual recognizes himself as an integral part of a social whole.[12]

Those who possessed such a common culture Herder called a *Volk*, and its principal identifying feature was its language. Common language for Herder has some of the attributes of Rousseau's 'general will' but, unlike the latter, it is an historical institution which can be studied empirically.

Herder provides a link with the earlier writers, whom we have considered. He found Father Lafitau's comparison of the habits of the Iroquois Indians and of the ancient Greeks of great interest, 'as a compendium of the ethics and poetics of savages'.[13] He studied the works of the Scottish writers such as Smith and Millar, and reviewed Millar's *Origin of Ranks* at length, observing, however, that his purely empirical approach was inadequate.[14] He was prepared to see political change in his own country but he wanted it to be 'gradual, natural, reasonable evolution', which took

---

[11] 'Reflections on the Revolution in France' (1790), *Works*, ed. H. Rogers (2 vols., London, 1852), 1.417.
[12] F. M. Barnard, *Herder on Social and Political Culture* (Cambridge, 1969), 7.
[13] Lafitau, *Customs*, ed. W. N. Fenton and E. L. Moore, Champlain Society (2 vols., Toronto, 1974), 1.cvii.
[14] *Sämtliche Werke* (Berlin, 1877), v.452–6, cited by Lehmann, *John Millar of Glasgow*, 156.

full account of the cultural character of the nation. He too used the metaphor of organism to describe the nation and its growth.

Savigny blended Hugo's historical approach to law with Burke's political conservatism and Herder's conception of the nation as a cultural entity characterised by its language and literature. The programme of his school was set out in his famous pamphlet, *Zum Beruf unsrer Zeit für Gesetzgebung und Rechtswissenschaft*,[15] published in 1814.

Napoleon, using his Civil Code, in Savigny's words, as a bond the more to fetter nations, imposed it on all the states of Germany which he had subjected to his rule. On his overthrow in 1814, it remained in force in some parts of Germany, and in others was discarded as 'a badge of political degradation' (p. iv). What should be put in its place? Thibaut, a distinguished Heidelberg professor, proposed the adoption of a code, not, of course, a code based on revolutionary ideals like Napoleon's, but a code in the tradition of the natural law systems, like the Prussian Code of 1794 and the Austrian Code of 1811. Such a code would be a unifying factor for the German states and the opportunity was too good to miss. Savigny rejected the proposal and argued successfully for reversion to the old law, based on the Roman law, in those areas where there was no local code.

Claiming to enquire how law has actually developed 'among nations of the nobler races', Savigny announces that, 'in the earliest times to which authentic history extends, the law will be found to have already attained a fixed character, peculiar to the people, like their language, manners and constitution'. Indeed these phenomena are not really distinct attributes at all; they are facets of one whole, bound by 'the common conviction of the people, the kindred consciousness of an inward necessity, excluding all notion of an accidental and arbitrary origin' (p. 24). Savigny does not consider life in the state of nature. He expressly denies that history can tell us how these peculiar characteristics of nations originated in a pre-political society.

As soon as a nation becomes a nation, he says, the objects of its popular faith are its language and its law. Language attains a fixed

---

[15] Translated by Abraham Hayward as *On the Vocation of our Age for Legislation and Jurisprudence* (London, 1831).

determinate character by constant usage. Law at first is not formulated in abstract rules; rather it is manifested through special forms, symbolic acts, which create or extinguish rights and duties. These formal ritual acts by their familiarity create a popular prejudice in their favour and give the law its particular individuality. People consider them as part of their special way of life. They 'may be considered as the true grammar of law in this period' (p. 26).

The organic connection of law with the character of the people is preserved as societies develop, and Savigny conceives of the development of societies as a cyclical process of growth and decay. A nation is born, matures, declines and dies. Law is an inseparable part of the nation's life; so 'law grows with the growth, and strengthens with the strength of the people, and finally dies away as the nation loses its individuality' (p. 27).[16]

In the first period, the law is expressed directly in the practices of the people. It has no technical expression in general rules and there is no well defined logical method of applying them. As civilisation progresses, a distinct class of jurists appears, who now represent the people so far as the more technical parts of law – lawyers' law, as we might say – are concerned. Law now has a two-fold existence. The popular part, which Savigny calls political, and which is intelligible to the mass of the people, continues as part of the general life of the nation; while the technical part is a distinct discipline in the hands of the jurists. The line of demarcation between the two elements will vary in different societies and the political element will tend to be greater in republics than in monarchies. In declining periods of a nation, its law loses its popular attraction and becomes merely the property of a few experts; even the technical element decays. The message is that, whether the law is custom or jurisprudence, it is everywhere developed 'by internal silently operating powers, not by the arbitrary will of a lawgiver' (p. 30). Legal change is seen as an automatic process, quite divorced from the actions and intentions of individuals.

Savigny then discusses the requirements for a successful code, and concludes that very few ages will be found qualified to make

[16] Hayward translates 'Eigentümlichkeit' as 'nationality', but 'individuality' seems more appropriate; E. Bodenheimer, *Jurisprudence* (Cambridge, Mass., 1962), 72, n. 6.

one. In their early periods nations have the clearest perception of their law but the technical element is inadequate so that their attempts at codification 'are defective in language and logical skill, and they are generally incapable of expressing what is best'. The Roman Twelve Tables and the medieval Germanic laws exemplify this. In declining ages, almost everything is lacking for a successful code, 'knowledge of the matter, as well as language', so that period is manifestly not the time for codification. The only possible period is the middle period, which marks the peak of a nation's cultural development; it has the maximum popular participation in the political element and the culmination of technical expertise among the jurists. 'But such an age has no need of a code for itself: it would merely compose one for a succeeding and less fortunate age, as we lay up provisions for the winter. But an age is seldom disposed to be so provident for posterity' (p. 42).

Having sketched his views on the development of law in societies, Savigny has to apply them first to Roman law and then to German law. The law of Justinian, which is the form in which Roman law has been transmitted to modern Europe, is the law of a period of decline. We must look to the classical period, the age of the great jurists, to see Roman law in its maturity. The greatness of the jurists, in Savigny's view, lay in their common possession of the leading principles of the law. Their whole mode of proceeding has a certainty which is found nowhere else, except in mathematics. They all reasoned in the same way from a common set of principles. The method is common to all; far from engaging in polemics, 'they all co-operate, as it were, in one and the same great work' (p. 45). The materials on which they worked were handed down to them from the time of the Republic. What made Rome great was the adaptability which made her introduce new institutions without jettisoning the old – 'a judicious mixture of the permanent and progressive principles' (p. 48).

Roman law shows that as long as the law was in active progression, no code was considered necessary, even when circumstances were most favourable for it. 'And when, in the sixth century, all intellectual life was dead, the wrecks of better times were collected to supply the demand of the moment' (p. 51).

Applying his scheme to the development of German law,

Savigny faced certain problems. First, how was it that the Germans in the late Middle Ages abandoned German law and accepted as the main source of German common law the law of Justinian, which was foreign and alien? He seeks to show that Roman law was received because of an internal necessity. Law, he says, can no more be an exclusive national possession than religion or literature. In any case the nomadic character of the Germanic tribes had deprived Germanic custom of any territorial focus. There was an interruption in the national development of the German people. When the feudal system was established, nothing peculiar to the old Germans was left; everything was changed by the time the Roman law was adopted. There was no alternative.

The next problem was, if the Germans were one people, how could one account for the multiplicity of laws in the various states? Here Savigny refers to the organic model. 'The well-being of every organic being (consequently of states) depends on the maintenance of an equipoise between the whole and its parts...a lively affection for the whole can only proceed from the thorough participation in all particular relations' (p. 58). So the particular laws of the various states are not obstacles to progress: in so far as they are more likely to be closer to the feelings and consciousness of the people, they are in fact an advantage.

Pointing out that Prussia and Austria had recently acquired codes of their own, Savigny then turns his argument round, and says that it would obviously lead to great confusion if these codes were repealed in favour of a new code for all. Presumably, therefore, the new German code, proposed by Thibaut, would apply only to the remaining German states, whose law was still uncodified, and in that case it would not achieve its object of being a code of law for the whole German people.

The pamphlet of 1814 was primarily a polemical work. If we examine Savigny's ideas carefully, we find that his scheme of law, emerging as part of the life of the people, and then being developed by jurists, was in no sense derived from evidence of what happens generally. It was an ideal scheme of legal development, which properly applied only to Roman law. Savigny admits as much when he assumes for it 'a complete undisturbed, national (*einheimische*) development' (p. 30). Roman law had such a development, as

Gibbon showed. German law did not have it, as Savigny admitted, and it required the incorporation of much Roman law into German law to get over the problems caused by the interruptions in its progress.

In fact, for Savigny, Roman law stood above and apart from other legal systems as a model, and he spent much effort in separating the pure Roman law from non-Roman (mainly German) adulteration. Savigny's scheme of legal evolution was inadequate, because it was a generalisation of a Roman model, which did not really apply to the German experience, and yet the only illustrations of his scheme that he offered were Roman law and German law. This defect notwithstanding, his basic idea was taken up with enthusiasm by his school. It was widely accepted that there is an organic and inevitable connection between law and the special character of a people.

Savigny had produced something for everybody.[17] The princes were pleased, because he gave them a defence against popular demands for radical reform legislation. The democrats were at least mollified by the assurance that law came from the people, not from princes. The professors were encouraged by the emphasis on their special responsibility as jurists to develop the law in its technical aspects and by the idea that the judges were to follow their expert findings. The nationalists were delighted by the stress laid on the particular character of the German people and its law.

It is not surprising that the German historical school split into two groups, Romanists and Germanists, each of which was charged with intense and romantic emotion. Maitland as usual put his finger on the mainspring of the Germanist historical movement when he said: 'every scrap and fragment of old German law was to be lovingly and scientifically recovered and edited. Whatever was German was to be traced through all its fortunes to its fount. The motive force in this prolonged effort...was not antiquarian pedantry, nor was it a purely disinterested curiosity. If there was science, there was also love.'[18]

In the hands of Savigny's followers, the historical school took

---

[17] H. Kantorowicz, 'Savigny and the Historical School of Law', *Law Quarterly Review*, 53 (1937), 336–7.

[18] Introduction to O. Gierke, *Political Theories of the Middle Ages* (Cambridge, 1900), xvi.

on an even more mystical and romantic quality than he gave it. The watchword of the school became the *Volksgeist*, the spirit of the people, which sounded like the spirit evoked by Montesquieu, but was in fact very different. For Montesquieu, the spirit of a nation was an amalgam of various specific components, climate, geography, religion, social customs and so on. For the followers of Savigny, it was a much vaguer, more intangible idea. Romantics everywhere felt in sympathy with it. Savigny's English translator notes that friends, to whom he showed his translation, were struck by the similarity between Savigny's cast of mind and that of Coleridge, expressed in his essay 'On the Constitution of the Church and State', in which he wrote of the tension between the powers of permanence and progression (*Vocation*, 48).

Hugo had welcomed the appearance of Savigny's 1814 pamphlet against Thibaut, and approved its emphasis on the importance of customary law and practice, and its attack on the supremacy of legislation. He supported Savigny's rejection of the currently prevailing view that 'legislation, and jurisprudence as well, are of wholly accidental and fluctuating nature; and it is very possible that the law of tomorrow may not at all resemble the law of today' (*Vocation*, 23). But Hugo was suspicious of the *Volksgeist*.[19] His empirical inclinations warned him that it was essentially unhistorical, in that it was based on an idea rather than on the facts of social life. Furthermore, Hugo had a vision of the future quite alien to Savigny. He envisaged the possibility of a world state and of an economic order without private property, so that he was not so concerned to preserve the existing order from reform.

Apart from its mystical quality, Savigny's doctrine tended to be conservative, in that it discouraged reform of the law by legislation. Twenty-five years after the publication of the pamphlet, in the introduction to his *System des Heutigen Römischen Rechts*, Savigny defended himself against the charge of fatalism: 'The existing matter will be injurious to us, so long as we ignorantly submit to it; but beneficial if we oppose to it a vivid creative energy – obtain the mastery over it by a thorough grounding in history, and thus appropriate to ourselves the whole intellectual wealth of preceding

[19] Review of Savigny's *System des Heutigen Römischen Rechts*, *Göttingische Gelehrte Anzeigen* (1840), 1019–20.

generations.' As W. Friedmann comments, 'This belated defence could not mitigate the effect of the doctrine which, at a time when social developments made the use of legislative energy more important than ever, looked backwards rather than forwards.'[20]

JHERING

Even those German writers who were not followers of Savigny were, however, affected by the climate of opinion which he created. The other giant figure, who bestrides nineteenth-century German legal scholarship with Savigny, is Rudolf von Jhering (1818–92).[21] Like Savigny, Jhering built up a legal philosophy out of a study of the development of Roman law, and in the mood of the times sought to identify its 'spirit'. His great work, significantly entitled *Der Geist des Römischen Rechts*,[22] of which the first volume was published in 1852, was designed to show the particular features of Roman law in the different periods of its history.

In the introduction, Jhering takes Savigny to task on two main counts. First, in regard to his theory of the national character of law, he points out that logically this is a condemnation of the presence of Roman law in the modern German state, as something alien to its national character. It is asserted that Roman law has become 'our law'. But how can this possibly be justified? In effect the reception of Roman law in Germany is incompatible with Savigny's premises. Jhering then demolishes the theory of the peculiar national spirit, which must at all costs be preserved from contamination, by arguing that, on the contrary, 'the prosperity of a people consists of an uninterrupted succession of foreign elements... Its particular character, like the physical and intellec-

---

[20] *Legal Theory*, 5th edn (London, 1967), 212, n. 9.
[21] Wieacker, *Privatrechtsgeschichte*, 450–3; Wieacker, *Gründer und Bewahrer*, 197–212; Wolf, *Grosse Rechtsdenker*, 622–68; J. Gaudemet, 'Organicisme et évolution dans la conception de l'histoire du droit chez Jhering', *Jherings Erbe*, ed. F. Wieacker and C. Wollschläger (*Abhandlungen der Akademie der Wissenschaften in Göttingen*, Phil.-hist. Kl., III folge, Nr. 75) (Göttingen, 1970), 29–39; G. Marini, 'La storicità del diritto e la scienza giuridica nel pensiero di Jhering', *ibid.*, 155–64.
[22] French translation by O. Meulenaere, 3rd edn (4 vols., Paris, 1886–8). An English translation is lacking, although B. T. C[rump] published a translation of the Preface under the title 'The Value of the Roman Law to the Modern World', *Virginia Law Journal*, 4 (1880), 453–64.

tual organism of the individual, is the product of innumerable imprints imposed by the outside world' (Introd. 1.1; Fr. tr. 1.8). The strength of Roman law, he observes, derives from its capacity to assimilate institutions and ideas from outside. At an early stage in its history it incorporates the rules of the *ius gentium*, rules regarded as common to all peoples and suggested by common sense, to supplement those of the *ius civile*, which was peculiar to Roman citizens. This readiness of Roman law to accept ideas which were originally foreign to it shows that a progressive law is characterised not by nationality but universality.

Secondly, Jhering criticises Savigny for his emphasis on the methods of the Roman jurists rather than on the content of the rules which they produced. The importance of the Roman law sources lies in the discussions of the jurists, and Savigny found the special feature of the juristic method to reside in the mathematical precision with which the Roman jurists applied principles to cases. Jhering argues that this means that the value of Roman law is made to depend on the accidental form in which Justinian happens to have transmitted the bulk of Roman law, namely in the anthology of extracts from the writings of the jurists, which constitutes the Digest. But this is purely a matter of form, and to stress the juristic technique is to ignore the other factors which contributed to fixing the value of Roman law. In Savigny's view, says Jhering, if Justinian's compilers had produced a modern code and not transmitted the texts of the Digest, we would have lost Roman law, whereas it is the essential substance of Roman law which has passed into modern legal systems and it is the quality of its rules which gives Roman law its value (Introd. 1.2; Fr. tr. 1.19).

Jhering stressed that the roots of the law were in actual social life and he rejected theories which compared jurisprudence with mathematics:

Let us rid ourselves of these prejudices which hold us captive. This desire for logic that turns jurisprudence into legal mathematics is an error and arises from misunderstanding law. Life does not exist for the sake of concepts, but concepts for the sake of life. It is not logic that is entitled to exist, but what is claimed by life, by social relations, by the sense of justice – and the logical necessity, or logical impossibility, is immaterial. One could have considered the Romans mad, if they had ever thought otherwise, if they had sacrificed the interests of life to the dialectics of the school (II.2. introd. 69; Fr. tr. IV.311).

Despite his down to earth criticism of Savigny's flights of fancy, Jhering still accepted that law is organic, that it is like a people's language, the internal product of a people's history. He spoke of the anatomy and physiology of law. Furthermore he did not deny a role to national character in determining the way the law develops. Like Savigny he selected for special praise those peoples who enjoy a finely balanced appreciation of conservative and progressive forces.

The more easy rapid and copious the production of law in a state, the feebler is its moral force. The longer the interval between conception and birth of a rule and the greater the pains of childbirth, the more solid and robust is the fruit. So law can only prosper among a people with a strong will. For it is only with such a people, that conservative and progressive forces have the degree of perfection for the law to progress slowly but surely; witness ancient Rome and England. Unhappily there are only too many examples to the contrary (Introd. 2.2.5; Fr. tr. 1.71).

Jhering accepted the basic idea of legal evolution but he recognised it to be a more complicated process than Savigny had represented it to be. The progress of law is not merely the result of unconscious growth, conditioned by innate popular character. That has its place, but legal development also depends on the conscious efforts of lawyers to solve the problems of social life. In the course of writing the third volume of his treatise, he says, he discovered that a legal right is really a legally protected interest, and this discovery led him to look for the purposes of law. He realised that law is directed to achieve certain aims, and consequently it is oriented to the future as much as to the past. The historical school had not adequately recognised these conscious struggles to achieve certain ends through law.

The aims of law are, however, more prominent at some periods than at others. In his study of Rome, Jhering accepted the contrast between the half-religious formalism and commonsense equity which characterises popular law in early periods, and the subtler methods of the professional jurist in later periods. He drew the conclusion that in early periods the law grows more or less organically, like language, whereas in later and more advanced stages, universal conceptions replace national ones, and legal institutions, like coins of standard value, circulate from country to country. Thus in progressive societies the law becomes less national and more universal as it develops, the most universal being, of course, Roman law. In his later work Jhering moved further away from evolution, and applied all his eloquence to a functionalist theory of law.

> Law is not less a product of history than handicraft, naval construction, technical skill: as Nature did not provide Adam's soul with a ready made conception of a kettle, of a ship or of a steamer, even so she has not presented him with property, marriage, binding contracts, the State. And the same may be said of all moral rules... The whole moral order is a product of history, or to put it more definitely, of the striving towards ends, of the untiring activity and work of human reason tending to satisfy wants and to provide against difficulties.[23]

The work from which that quotation is taken was described by contemporary Germans as 'German Benthamism', and in his later writings, Jhering's original historical bias was modified considerably by Bentham's ideas.[24] It is to Bentham's England that we must at this point retrace our steps.

---

[23] *Der Zweck im Recht*, II (Leipzig, 1883), 112, as cited by P. Vinogradoff, *Outlines of Historical Jurisprudence* (2 vols., Oxford, 1920–2), I.137.

[24] H. Coing, 'Benthams Bedeutung für die Entwicklung der Interessenjurisprudenz und der allgemeinen Rechtslehre', *Archiv für Rechts- und Sozial-philosophie*, 54 (1968), 69–88; cf. J. H. Drake, preface to Jhering, *Law as a means to an end* (translation of vol. I of *Der Zweck im Recht*) (Boston, 1913), xvii–xxi.

4

The heyday of legal evolution

The situation in England was quite different from that in Germany, and to a continental observer was quite unintelligible. In 1831 Savigny wrote to his English translator, Abraham Hayward, that he had been for long pained that 'your country in all other branches of knowledge actively communicating with the rest of the world, should, in jurisprudence alone, have remained divided from the rest of the world, as if by a Chinese wall'.[1]

In Germany the prevailing view at the opening of the nineteenth century was that enforceable law was essentially statute law, emanating from the ruler as legislator. In England the prevailing view was still that enshrined in Blackstone's *Commentaries on the Laws of England* of 1765: the law was essentially common law, which was ancient custom, refined over the centuries by the practical reason which resided in the capacious bosoms of the king's justices. When the occasion arose in a particular case, parts of this law were declared to the world in their judgements, and might eventually appear in the law reports, but it was never finally stated anywhere. Thus when Jeremy Bentham argued that law was what the legislator commanded in statutes (a sentiment which would have been quite unexceptionable in Germany, as Hugo complained), he was attacking the dominant opinion and advocating what in England was a most unorthodox view.

[1] *A Selection from the Correspondence of A. Hayward*, ed. H. E. Carlisle (London, 1886), 15.

BENTHAM AND AUSTIN

Bentham totally rejected the tradition symbolised by Blackstone, who had extolled the common law as the perfection of reason, brought to the pitch of perfection by the practice of the judges.[2] Bentham argued that the common law was imaginary law made up by the judges for each particular occasion. Before it is applied, no one knows what it is, not even the lawyers. It is dog law: 'When your dog does anything you want to break him of, you wait till he does it and then beat him for it...this is the way the judges make law for you and me.'[3] Blackstone was justifying the assumption of arbitrary power by the judges. Law is not what the judges say but is rather the expressed will of the legislator, following the principle of utility by maximising happiness and reducing the incidence of pain. Law lays down what the citizen should do, and the citizen must know the effects of his conduct before he acts. The only true law is statute law.

So far as legal change was concerned, Bentham's attitude was that this should be made expressly and rationally by legislators who had been trained, preferably by himself, for the purpose. In this regard he presented himself as the prophet of moderation, who was concerned to maintain public trust and confidence in the legal system. The man

> who should be so confined in his views, or so unreasonable in his ideas of reform, as to seek to inspire revolt or contempt against the general system of the laws, would be unworthy of attention at the tribunal of an enlightened public, who can enumerate their benefits – I do not say under the best, but under the worst of governments...Innovations in the laws should be made with great caution. It is not well to destroy everything, upon pretence of reconstructing the whole: the fabric of the laws may be easily dilapidated, but it is difficult to be repaired, and its alteration ought not to be entrusted to rash and ignorant operators (*Works*, I.326).

Bentham's influence on the substantive law was more dramatic than his influence on legal theory, partly because there was very little writing which could properly be called legal theory. Reform legislation proceeded at an unprecedented pace from the 1820s onwards. Parliament was reformed, the franchise extended, and the

---

[2] P. Stein, 'Il sorgere del movimento analitico–positivistico in Inghilterra', *Studi Senesi*, 3rd series, 19 (1970), 319–39.
[3] *Works*, ed. J. Bowring (11 vols., Edinburgh, 1843), v.234.

consequent transfer of political power from the aristocracy to the middle class was accompanied by much humanitarian legislation, such as the Factories Acts, and the statutes reforming the brutality of the penal system. In every area of law, reform was the order of the day and reform was synonymous with Bentham. In 1828, Henry Brougham told Parliament, 'The age of law reform and the age of Jeremy Bentham are one and the same. He is the father of the most important of all the branches of reform, the leading and ruling department of human improvement. No one before him had ever seriously thought of exposing the defects of our English jurisprudence.'[4] And in 1874 Sir Henry Maine, by no means an uncritical admirer, wrote, 'I do not know of a single law reform effected since Bentham's day which cannot be traced to his influence.'[5]

In the period after the Napoleonic wars, Bentham's ideas directly stimulated proposals to codify English law;[6] much of his legal theory was, however, popularised more by his devoted disciple, John Austin, than by himself. Austin was Professor of Jurisprudence at University College, London, for a few years in the 1820s, before he became disheartened by the lack of interest in legal education and ceased to lecture. To prepare himself for his work, he studied law in Germany. There he was impressed by the systematic, logical treatises of modernised Roman law produced by the early Pandectists, one of the most prominent of whom was Savigny's adversary, Thibaut. These works were much influenced by the natural law systems of the eighteenth century and set out the whole law as a clear and coherent body of principles and rules. The Roman law, in the form in which it was dressed by the German Pandectists, was in Austin's view 'greatly and palpably superior, considered as a system or whole, to the law of England. Turning from the study of the English to the study of the Roman law, you escape from the empire of chaos and darkness to a world which seems by comparison, the region of order and light.'[7]

[4] Cited by A. V. Dicey, *Law and Public Opinion in England during the nineteenth century*, 2nd edn (London, 1914), 126–7.
[5] *Lectures on the Early History of Institutions*, 7th edn (London, 1905), 397.
[6] W. Teubner, *Kodifikation und Rechtsreform in England* (Berlin, 1974), 144ff.
[7] *Lectures on Jurisprudence*, 5th edn by R. Campbell (London, 1885), 58; cf. A. B. Schwarz, 'John Austin and the German jurisprudence of his time', *Politica*, 1 (1934), 178, and (in German) in Schwarz, *Rechtsgeschichte und Gegenwart* (Karlsruhe, 1960), 73ff.

Austin argued that the province of jurisprudence was positive law, which was 'law set by political superiors to political inferiors' (Lecture 1). Its validity was determined by the fact that it was commanded by the sovereign person or body in the society, whom Austin identified as that habitually obeyed by the bulk of the population. Most of his work was directed to the analysis of the legal notions which were common to English law and the Pandectist form of Roman law, for he assumed that concepts found in these two systems were universally applicable.

The ideas of Bentham and Austin attracted an enthusiastic following among liberal thinkers who favoured law reform. Those who opposed them had to find respectable counter-arguments. They concentrated on the failure of the Benthamites to give adequate consideration to historical factors. They could have used the arguments of the Scottish historical school but these were viewed with some suspicion, since a number of their proponents, especially Millar, were regarded as radicals who favoured the French Revolution. Savigny and his school were more conservative; their arguments were specifically addressed to the issue of codification, and they stressed the special character of each nation in a reassuring way.

THE INFLUENCE OF SAVIGNY

Some of these opponents of Bentham had acquired their knowledge of Savigny's ideas in Germany. J. J. Park (1795–1833) had taken a doctorate in law at Göttingen. In 1828 he published an attack on certain proposals for partial codification under the title *A Contra Project to the Humphreysian Code and to the projects of reduction by Messrs Hammond, Uniacke and Twiss*, in which he stressed the particular historical independence of English law, and the inorganic nature of the reforms proposed. Three years later Park became a Professor of Law at Kings College, London, but died shortly afterwards.[8]

---

[8] Another barrister who was at this period familiar with the German historical school as arguing against codification, was C. P. Cooper (1793–1873). See his *Lettres sur la cour de la Chancellerie d'Angleterre, et sur quelques points de la jurisprudence anglaise* (London, 1828; 2nd edn Paris, 1830) (esp. 1828 edn, pp. vii–viii and 1830 edn, pp. 347–72), and

The first full statement in English of the ideas of the German historical school was published in London, in the same year as Park's essay, by another Göttingen graduate, the Scotsman John Reddie. In his *Letter to the Lord High Chancellor of Great Britain on the expediency of the Proposal to form a new civil code for England*, he gives an account of legal development which is pure Savigny.[9] The following extracts give some idea of Reddie's approach:

> The first link of the great chain of law, is formed by custom, and usage, and the adoption of those rules which instinctive expediency suggests. In the course of time, and according to the peculiarities of each country, through the intercourse of man with his fellow men, a Consuetudinary jurisprudence develops itself, suited to the genius – because it sprung from that genius – of the nation amongst whom it has arisen... As circumstances, habit, or inclination, happen to prevail, each nation involuntarily and insensibly, adopts different, but appropriate, and according to her situation, necessary views of national justice. As manners change, laws change with them; and the latter keep pace with, whilst they aid the advancement, and receive their impress from the former. Those views and customs which, in process of time, are converted into formal laws, have grown from some natural, because nationally operating feeling; and they have unfolded themselves along with the ideas of the people, a part of whose character they form. For laws are nationally individual, and are as characteristically peculiar to the people, amongst whom they arise, as their religion, or language. And although their origin may sometimes be lost in the remoteness of tradition, yet it is based upon the most stable foundation – the spontaneous involuntary acknowledgment of the nation (pp. 5–6).

> All law emanates from the people

> and it is the conviction of their expediency, of their absolute necessity, for the preservation and welfare of society, which excludes all idea of an arbitrary origin, and bestows, upon human customs, and institutions, the stability and stamp of nature.

> In the more advanced periods of civilisation, when a regular government – no matter of what description – has been established, the Legislature, the Judges, and the Lawyers, are but the organs of the nation; they merely fix the limits, and connexion between, the various principles and rules which have thus arisen. It is the genius of the people that gives birth to, and animates the system, which is elucidated, and technically arranged by the lawyers, and, through their labours, becomes a science (pp. 6–7).

> In every nation, where civil jurisprudence has attained to any degree of refinement, the strictness and severity of its positive enactments, have been

---

Brief Account of some of the most important proceedings in Parliament, relative to the defects in the administration of justice in the Court of Chancery (London, 1828), appendix C. I am grateful to Professor J. H. Burns for these references.

[9] Although the only source directly cited is the *Exposé Systématique des Lois de l'Empire Russe*, published by the Legislative Commission of St Petersburg.

mitigated, and suited to the extension and progress of society, by Equity – in Rome, by the institution of the Praetors, in England by the Court of Chancery. And the main body of the Laws, are from time to time altered, or added to by the Legislature, according as the changes are required by the altering circumstances of the nation. Thus, the law is always in a continually progressive state of existence. From what formerly was valid as law, that which now is, has emanated; the one has grown out of the other, and exists as law, because the other has ceased to be law. In the centuries of past ages lies the root of that magnificent tree, under whose protecting branches, the monarch, and the peasant, alike find shelter and repose (p. 8).

All Civil Laws then, in the most comprehensive sense of the term, even in the most refined and artificial age, are to be referred to three sources; to usage; to statutory enactment, sometimes fixing, sometimes altering usage; and to the decisions of the judges, extending, expounding, and applying, both the former. But to trace their distinct and separate origin is often impossible; for established customs, statutes, and judicial determinations, act and react upon each other; and even effects become causes, in their subsequent operation.

Thus the course of jurisprudence is never stationary; it is either on the ebb, or on the flow; and although the current may in some places roll with a greater velocity, and, to the eye, with a more apparent stream, yet whether it expand itself with a fertilizing activity over the extensive plain, or is confined within narrow and shelving banks, the same portion of element issues to the ocean.

In short, the law of any nation is a part of the character of the people (p. 9).

After the publication of Hayward's translation of Savigny's pamphlet in 1831 the ideas of the historical school became more familiar to Englishmen interested in general legal issues. An important contribution to the codification debate in England was the article on Legislation in the seventh edition of the *Encyclopaedia Britannica*, published in 1842. It was written by William Empson (1791–1852), a regular contributor to, and later editor of, the *Edinburgh Review*, who was 'professor of general polity and the laws of England' at the East India College, Haileybury. He was generally in favour of codification and tried to counter the academic arguments with which it was being opposed, especially the claim that it was unhistorical.

In the opening section he cites Adam Smith and refers to the enormous differences between societies. 'Montesquieu's Spirit of the Laws, and the Treatise on Legislation by M. Comte, are excellent repertories of the principal facts by which travellers have established the variety that exists among the families of the human species scattered over the globe.' He then observes that Edmund Burke acknowledged his debt to Robertson's *History of America* for furthering our understanding of human nature by his account of the way of life of the American Indians. But Burke had added that 'we need no longer go to history to trace it in all stages and periods'. Indeed such was our knowledge of different societies, that we might understand human nature better comparatively than historically, for 'the great map of mankind is unrolled at once and there is no state or gradation of barbarism, and no mode of refinement which we have not at the same moment under our view: the very different civility of Europe and of China; the barbarism of Persia and of Abyssinia; the erratic manners of Tartary and of Arabia; the savage state of North America and of New Zealand' (XIII.167).

Empson tries to neutralise the objections of the historical school to codification, by arguing that Savigny's thesis in his 'celebrated essay' *On the Vocation of our Age*... was confined to Germany after the Napoleonic Wars and so had no general application. 'His very title significantly fixes the object of the work. It is addressed to the present age... Savigny's essay, at the time it was published, was a political pamphlet against the French. Prussia had just cleared her soil of their bayonets, and her tribunals of their laws... Savigny's pages are the exulting gratulations of an enthusiastic lawyer on the recovery of his country's legal freedom.' Indeed, when German jurisprudence has attained the qualities necessary for good legislation, Savigny contemplates the possibility of codification of German law and the consequent 'euthanasia of the historical school' (XIII.196-7).

By the mid-1840s it was generally recognised that there were two opposing schools of legal thinking, the historical school and the analytical school, the latter composed of utilitarian codifiers. Some writers saw them as extremes which could perhaps be brought closer together. In 1840, James Reddie, the father of John Reddie, summed up the merits and shortcomings of the historical school in a single enormous sentence of his *Inquiries, elementary and historical, in the Science of Law*:

But while it is thus conceded to the historical school, that with a view to effecting salutary changes, and real meliorations in the laws of a people, a profound knowledge of their history, of the physical, moral, religious, and legal, or juridical states through which they have passed, is an indispensable requisite, the leaders of that school ought, at the same time, to have distinctly admitted, that such profound knowledge of the actual and previous states of a people, can only be turned to practical account, and made beneficial by its combination with a philosophical analysis of the principles of the human constitution, as exhibited in the intercourse of mankind as divided into, and united in separate communities or states; and that the improvement of law, which arises naturally, and almost necessarily from the education or instruction which each generation imparts to its successor, may be greatly accelerated by the exertions of a wise and enlightened government, in gradually adapting the laws, which have come to be established, to the changes which may have taken place, in the circumstances, views, and feelings of the nation; in abrogating rules and usages, which are no longer necessary or useful; in shortening cumbrous processes in the law, and in simplifying and scientifically arranging the system.

The jurists of the analytical school, on the other hand, overrated the advantages for legal science of enunciating the principle of utility.

They seem to despise the instruction to be derived by the legislator from the experience of past ages, as recorded in history. In their excessive generalization, as remarked by M. Savigny and M. Comte, they divest law of its actual, individual, or particular character, of its national originality, and appear to consider it as composed of inflexible abstractions, like the mathematical sciences. They neglect those views of the historical school, with reference to the previous, and present, states of a people, which are indispensably necessary, to secure the introduction, and salutary establishment of any system of laws, however metaphysically complete it may be otherwise, or perfect in itself (pp. 90–1).

The association of Savigny and Comte is interesting, since it shows that Savigny was seen as a social evolutionist. Auguste Comte's *Cours de philosophie positive* (6 vols., 1830–42)[10] gained a wide following among English intellectuals. Comte offered a comprehensive 'scientific' conception of the world and of man. He held that the human mind passes through three stages in its quest for scientific understanding: first, theological, in which understanding of phenomena is in terms of anthropomorphic gods; secondly, metaphysical, when it is in terms of philosophical abstractions; and thirdly positive, when finally it can attain scientific truth. Comte regarded his three stages of human understanding as a fundamental law of mental evolution, and supported the doctrine by a detailed, although rather arbitrary, history of scientific ideas. Only when the human mind reached the third stage was it capable of scientific understanding. This occurred with

[10] An abbreviated English translation by Harriet Martineau (2 vols., London, 1853).

different disciplines at different times, the order being based on their decreasing generality and increasing complexity and detail. The positive method thus moved from mathematics through physics and chemistry to sociology (a word invented by Comte), which was the last science to reach the positive stage.

Sociology was to reveal the laws governing social life and controlling the way it evolved. For Comte held a progressive view of society and sometimes seemed to envisage it as advancing inexorably by a series of necessarily determined stages to some never-quite-to-be-attained goal. He spoke of the science of the necessary and continuous movement of humanity. Montesquieu, he considered, condescendingly, had made a good effort at presenting the elements of social evolution but he was premature since in his day society had not yet been studied by the positive method (*Cours*, IV.299). Comte was not completely determinist, but he strictly limited the power of political activity to control the changes which take place by mere force of circumstances. In general, history was the application of natural laws of progress.[11]

English writers related the positive method to the Baconian inductive method, which they regarded as its prototype. But their concern, in John Stuart Mill's words, was with 'the laws according to which any state of society produces the state which succeeds it and takes its place. This opens the great and vexed question of the progressiveness of man and society; an idea involved in every just conception of social phenomena as the subject of a science.'[12] As John Burrow, in citing this passage, neatly comments, 'The result is an emphasis on the detection of laws of social change at the expense of the study of social systems.'[13] In this climate of thought, Savigny's school could be seen as being concerned with the natural laws governing legal change in progressive societies.

In the 1840s and 1850s an historian who sought to be more than a mere antiquarian, and to attain a scientific understanding, modelled his techniques on those of the natural sciences. The greatest example of an historical work in this mode is George Grote's *History of Greece*, the first volumes of which appeared in

[11] L. Levy-Bruhl, *The Philosophy of Auguste Comte*, ed. F. Harrison (London, 1903), 260.
[12] *A System of Logic* (1834), 9th edn (2 vols., London, 1875), II.510.
[13] *Evolution and Society* (Cambridge, 1966), 108.

1846. Grote expressly approved Comte's 'doctrine of the three successive stages of the human mind in reference to scientific study', which he said was 're-stated and elucidated' by John Stuart Mill in his *System of Logic*. He observed that the early Greek philosophers, 'when they ceased to follow the primitive instinct of tracing the phaenomena of nature to personal and designing agents, passed over, not at once to induction and observation, but to a misemployment of abstract words, substituting metaphysical *eidôla* in the place of polytheism, and to an exaggerated application of certain narrow physical theories'. Grote points out that 'nothing else could be expected from the scanty stock of facts then accessible, and that the most profound study of the human mind [i.e. Comte's] points out such transition as an inevitable law of intellectual progress' (1.496–7).

John Conington, reviewing the early volumes of the *History of Greece* in the *Edinburgh Review* in 1851, noted a similarity between Grote's method and that of Francis Bacon, and continued:

It is no mere arbitrary connexion of thought which leads us to associate Mr Grote's name with that of the great father of modern inductive philosophy. The conception of a scientific treatment of history is as yet so little understood, much less admitted, in England, that we almost seem to require an apology for venturing to characterise the present work as the first attempt which has been made within our knowledge, at least by an Englishman, to deal with history in the concrete as a portion of science. Mr Grote, it is true, does not expressly speak of himself as desiring to regard his subject in this light; but it is sufficiently apparent that he recognises it both in theory and in practice. His general philosophy is evidently that of the positive school, as represented by M. Comte in France and by Mr J. S. Mill among ourselves, – men, whose greatest triumph is that they have been able to imagine a science of society and to indicate the conditions, whether practicable or not, under which its existence is conceivable (XCIV.207).

THE COMMITTEE ON LEGAL EDUCATION

In 1846, the House of Commons set up a Select Committee on Legal Education which reported quite simply that 'no Legal Education, worthy of the name, of a public nature, is at this moment to be had' in either England or Ireland. This state of affairs exhibited 'a striking contrast and inferiority to such education, provided as it is with ample means, and a judicious system for their application, at present in operation in all the more civilised states of Europe and America'. In particular the

Committee deplored the lack, in the English Universities, of a legal education such as existed elsewhere, and the consequent absence of any literature on the scientific and philosophical aspects of law. As a result, England was 'deprived of a most important class, the Legists or Jurists of the Continent, men who, unembarrassed by the small practical interests of their profession, are enabled to apply themselves exclusively to Law as to a science'. The Committee recommended that 'an outline of the History and Progress of Law, with the Elements of Jurisprudence, from approved textbooks, might very advantageously form a portion of the Under-graduate's course'.[14] Their Report expressed a particular interest in German legal education, which was held up as an example that England might follow.

There was an immediate reaction to the Report, and efforts were made to remedy the calamitous state of affairs which it had revealed. Both the Universities and the Inns of Court took steps to provide a legal education of the scientific character required by the Report. The Middle Temple set up its own committee which recommended that 'the first step for the promotion of Legal Education to be taken by this House, should be the appointment of a Reader on Jurisprudence and the Civil Law', and George Long was appointed.

GEORGE LONG

Long had been a Cambridge classical scholar, who was appointed by Thomas Jefferson to be the first Professor of Ancient Languages at his new University of Virginia at Charlottesville, and who was later Professor of Latin at University College, London. He became interested in Roman law, and was called to the Bar in 1837. In his two inaugural lectures,[15] he explained the aims of the revived legal education. First, the systematic exposition of the principles of General Jurisprudence, in the sense of principles universally

[14] *Report from the Select Committee on Legal Education*, 25 August 1846, House of Commons Proceedings 686, conclusions, ss. 1, 3, 6 and 11; cf. P. Stein, 'Legal Theory and the Reform of Legal Education in mid-nineteenth century England', *L'Educazione Giuridica II: Profili storici*, ed. A. Giuliani and N. Picarda (Perugia, 1979), 185–206.

[15] *Two Discourses delivered in Middle Temple Hall* (London, 1847), reprinted in *Law Library*, 60 (Philadelphia, 1848).

recognised by all legal systems and grounded in human nature, 'a philosophy of positive morality and positive law'; and secondly, the study of civil law, by which the Middle Temple Committee intended 'what may be called Modern Roman Law, that is to say, those portions of the civil law which being of a universal character and applicable to the relations of modern society, have formed the basis of the jurisprudence of many continental nations, and entered so largely into our own' (pp. 5–6). Long explains that this study supplements the teaching of general jurisprudence 'by the consideration that the Roman law, by reason of its universality, approaches nearer to a system of general jurisprudence than any other' (p. 7).

There is, at first impression, an Austinian ring in the references to the philosophy of positive law and the universality of the modern Roman law. However, Long makes it clear that he has derived his material mainly from Savigny. In the three decades since the publication of his famous anti-codification pamphlet, Savigny had toned down some of the more polemical arguments of the historical school. His most recent work, that which was used by Long, was a systematic treatment of modern Roman law.[16] In the preface he claimed that the historical school did not deny validity to other scientific forms of jurisprudence, and that it was a misrepresentation of its view of law to suggest that the legal culture which has grown out of the past is something that must be preserved immutable in the future. Each age has to interpret the law for itself.

Long explains that the object of the new scientific legal education was to give the student a view of the whole of the law instead of merely certain fragments of it. Furthermore,

> one of the strongest arguments in favour of a body of public teachers, whose business it shall be to expound the whole of the law which we possess, is derived from the development and the change which all law must and does undergo in the course of time. We have two striking historical examples of this – the Roman law and our own. The Roman law had many centuries of growth, change, and progress. So long as the huge mass was impressed by the mental activity and sound practical sense of their great jurists, it was in the course of useful practical development. With the decay of this class of men and the contemporaneous

---

[16] *System des Heutigen Römischen Rechts* (Berlin, 1840), *ante*, p. 64. A poor English version of vol. 1 appeared as *System of Modern Roman Law*, translated by W. Holloway (Madras, 1867).

political disorganization of the empire improvement ceased, and all that we find afterwards was an attempt to preserve, by compilations, of little merit as such, the dismembered fragments of that to which the clear understandings of a Paulus, and Ulpian, or a Papinian, could alone give a vital coherence (pp. 34–5).

In a similar way English law has undergone great changes since the Norman conquest;

nor is it possible but that further changes must from time to time be made, as the social wants shall be more clearly developed, and new necessities shall arise...But in the midst of the overwhelming and incongruous mass of which the whole body of our law consists, we possess certain elements of order and improvement. We have had a long national existence, and our present condition has grown out of the past...Our present and our past are not disjoined by any rude separation, and we find ourselves in the nineteenth century with the experience of age and the vigour of youth (p. 36)

The important fact is that some nations have in the character of their people and in their political institutions the elements of development and progress and others have not (p. 47).

In his second discourse Long gives a most perceptive account of the development of Roman law in the Savigny manner. The Roman state in the late Republic and early Empire, he observes, had

abundant material for the production and elaboration of a large body of law, applicable to all the purposes of life, and to the condition of every civilized nation. But material may exist without being worked upon, just as a barbarous people may starve with all the elements of wealth around them. The Roman knew how to use what he possessed, and this power he derived from the native energy of his character and the free institutions under which he lived (pp. 52–3).

Roman law owes its high scientific elaboration to the jurists, but,

the jurists did not create; indeed they could not create the matter on which they laboured: it existed as a product of the long series of years during which the legal institutions of Rome had grown out of the wants of the people (p. 55). The development of Roman law was mainly due to the mode in which the law was administered; it owed comparatively little to direct legislation (p. 56). The merit of the Romans consisted in modifying, extending, and adapting a very narrow and rigorous system to the progressive wants of society; in keeping to the form and letter of the law as far as they could, and reconciling it with the change of circumstances (p. 66).

In this regard Long drew particular attention to the use of fictions to extend the scope of the early strict law. For example, a man

might not have obtained the legal ownership of a thing for want of having observed the necessary legal forms, but he might have complied with every other substantial condition. In such a case, if it were necessary, the Formula of the praetor would direct the judex to treat him as owner, and if he found the substantial facts of the case to be in his favour, to pronounce his judgement as if he were owner. Thus fictions were introduced, in devising which the Romans shewed no small ingenuity (p. 59).

Later another phase was inaugurated by the peregrine praetor, who dealt with cases involving foreigners. He introduced the rules regarded as *ius gentium*. 'It is to the extended intercourse of the Roman with other people, that we must attribute the development of that part of their system, which consisted in the admission of those rules which the common understanding of mankind in all ages, and in all countries, has recognised to be right or just, or equitable' (pp. 63–4).

So obvious was Long's dependence on Savigny that a reviewer of the *Discourses* felt obliged to utter a warning: 'Mr Long must take especial care not to be led by Savigny (to whose valuable work he expresses his obligations) into too abstract and Germanized a system of lecturing.'[17]

The revival of interest in Roman law, it was constantly repeated, was associated with its role in the new legal education, and here Savigny was the prophet of its universality. J. T. Abdy, Maine's successor as Regius Professor of Civil Law at Cambridge, put it neatly in the preface to his *Historical Sketch of Civil Procedure among the Romans*, published in 1857:

The study of Roman law will help to bring out that two-fold spirit which, to use Savigny's words, is indispensable to the jurist, the historical, by which the peculiarities of every age and every form of law may be seized and appreciated – the systematic, by which every nation and every rule may be placed in lively connection and co-operation with the whole.

MCLENNAN

The change in the character of the discussion of legal origins which took place around 1850 can best be illustrated by comparing the article on Law in the seventh edition of the *Encyclopaedia*

[17] *Law Magazine*, XXXVII (N.S. VI) (1847), 238. For German influence on English legal ideas, E. Campbell, 'German influences in English legal education and jurisprudence in the 19th century', *Univ. of West. Australia Ann. Law Review*, 4 (1959); C. H. S. Fifoot, *Judge and Jurist in the Reign of Victoria* (London, 1959), *passim*; P. Stein, 'Continental influences on English legal thought, 1600–1900', *Atti del III Congresso internazionale della Società italiana per la storia del diritto* (Florence, 1977), III.1120ff.

Britannica, published in 1842, with that in the eighth edition, which appeared in 1857. The former was little more than an abridgement of Blackstone's introduction to his *Commentaries*, although it was supplemented by the separate article on Legislation, to which reference has been made. The latter combined the two topics into one article and adopted an entirely new approach. It was written by J. F. McLennan, an archetypal Scots 'lad o'pairts' who was born in 1827 in Inverness, graduated from King's College, Aberdeen, was a mathematical Wrangler in 1853 at Cambridge (although for some reason he did not take his degree)[18] spent a couple of years in London and in 1857 was admitted to the Scots Bar in Edinburgh.

McLennan may be said to have done his homework for the article, which was his first published work. He cites Montesquieu, Adam Smith (*Theory of Moral Sentiments*), James and John Stuart Mill, Savigny (a substantial extract from *On the Vocation of our Age*) and Comte (the two are again treated together), and Grote. The thrust of the article is on evolution:

> The fulness of the idea of law has not been reached by the whole of any system of laws now administered; but in the progress of civilization, the tendency everywhere is towards its realization. Law is, and always has been, in a state of growth and development. History is clear that in the infancy of society men had no idea of regulating their relations on general or uniform principles, and that they knew no rules except such as their natural interconnection established, – a rude approach towards justice between equals; for the rest, the arbitrary rule of power over weakness. [In considering the progress of justice as against brute force] it is to be kept in view that rules of human action are due to the contact and clashing of men with men (XIII.255).

McLennan states that the causes of the progress of law are partly to be sought in the earliest stages of society, and that there is no satisfactory information on them. However some assistance may be gained from intelligent observers' accounts of savage societies, from international relations, which resemble a society in its early stages, from observation of any new society formed by its members for some purpose, and from observation of the development and

---

[18] P. Rivière, in his edition of *Primitive Marriage* (Chicago, 1970), viii, suggests that McLennan's failure to take his degree was the result of disappointment with his Tripos result. Since, as 25th Wrangler, he received First Class Honours, this is unlikely. Probably he was reluctant to take the Anglican religious test (abolished by the Cambridge University Act of 1856), then required as a condition of taking his B.A. degree.

tendencies of individuals. He rejects the idea that civil society was formed by agreement of individuals; it 'obviously commences in the family' and 'the state where the government is patriarchal is indeed the direct prolungation of the family'. The 'order of evolution of law' is that laws 'may be said to have first grown round the marriage relation, next round the institution of property; and, lastly, to have referred to the punishment of offences against the person. The right of private vengeance, and the insatiable character of revenge, long prevented the adoption of rules regarding punishment' (XIII.255–6).

Enumerating the sources from which law grows, McLennan seems to have collected a miscellaneous list from a variety of types of literature. First comes equity, which is a natural law idea. It proceeds from 'conceptions of right and wrong...generated by experience of, and reflection on, the realities of things, and what is convenient to them'. Next in order are decisions, and here McLennan relies on Grote's explanation of the earliest term for law in Greek, *themistes*, settlements of disputes by Zeus (in association with the goddess Themis), not as lawgiver, but as judge. These sources precede law; morality and law are not yet distinguished. The highest rudimentary form of true law is custom, based on what the bulk of the population approves. Finally there is legislation, which differs from the other sources in that 'from the sovereign's will law springs forth full-armed', whereas from the others law 'grows up slowly and organically' (XIII.256–7). It is a mistake to think that, once the stage of legislation is attained, law making is an entirely free exercise of the sovereign's will. For the sovereign is controlled by public opinion.

On this stage being reached, it would seem as if the original causes of the growth of law ceased to operate. But, in fact, their action has merely been changed from the direct to the indirect, for it is only by the concurrence of the individual wills of the people that the sovereign possesses his authority...The changes in the law, then, produced by legislative action are not to be regarded as being arbitrary, but as being, in the long run, the effect of the indirect action of the same causes as develop customary law (XIII.260).

Buried in the discussion of sources of law is an observation which seems to contain the germ of one of the most influential ideas in nineteenth-century legal theory. Discussing agreements for the arbitration of disputes, McLennan says: 'In proportion to the necessity for arbitration would be the desire to rule relationships by contract; and the desire to prevent differences by ruling relationships by contract would be greater the more they tended to give birth to differences. It is on this principle that the order of the evolution of law is to be explained' (XIII.257–8).

This enigmatic statement, when taken with the order of evolution itself, i.e. marriage, property, punishment of offences against the person, distinctly suggests that legal evolution is a progress from family relationships to individual contract.

Did McLennan derive this, and other ideas which anticipate Maine's *Ancient Law*, from his reading? It is possible that when he was in London, after leaving Cambridge in 1853, he attended lectures at the Inns of Court; and it was at that time that Maine began to lecture at the Middle Temple. Burrow hints that McLennan might have heard the lectures which we know contained much of the material of Maine's work.[19] On the other hand, we are told that while in London McLennan was occupied in journalism, and when he decided to study law, he did so in Edinburgh, where, as the Report of the 1846 Committee had admitted, legal education was in better shape than in England. Later in their lives, when McLennan championed the matriarchal theory against the patriarchal theory (held by Maine), which McLennan himself had adopted in the *Britannica* article, there was a certain antagonism between the two men, but never was it suggested that McLennan had taken over Maine's ideas. It seems more likely that the 1857 article reflects enlightened opinion in the circle of Grote, G. H. Lewes and John Stuart Mill in London, and the reading that was suggested to its author by them and by legal thinkers in Edinburgh. It contains more than a hint of the conjectural history of the Scottish enlightenment and a link with John Millar's ideas is quite possible.

In the same year, 1861, there appeared the two works which had greater influence on English jurisprudence than any other in the nineteenth century. One was the second edition of Austin's *Province of Jurisprudence Determined*, brought out by his widow after the author's death in 1859; and the other was Henry Maine's *Ancient Law*.

Austin's work was immediately welcomed as the only English

[19] *Evolution*, 230.

work which offered a methodology for the scientific textbooks on English law required by the new courses. In 1883, E. C. Clark wrote, 'After a life which had so little of the well-deserved success to balance so much disappointment and failure, the work of the dead Austin is achieving results beyond what even he would have anticipated. It is undoubtedly forming a school of English jurists... It is the staple of jurisprudence in all our systems of legal education.'[20] Our concern, however, must now be focussed on the other work of 1861, that of Henry Maine.

MAINE

Maine's work was also the product of a lecture course. After distinguishing himself as a classicist and as a member of the 'Apostles' (a group in the Cambridge tradition of those who 'know every thing, examine every thing and dogmatize about every thing')[21] Maine was appointed Regius Professor of Civil Law at Cambridge in 1847 at the age of twenty-five. He held the Chair for seven years until he took over the Middle Temple Readership, held earlier by George Long. His enthusiasm for the Roman law which it was his duty to teach was unbounded. In his first essay[22] he wrote: 'We are driven to admit that the Roman jurisprudence may be all that its least cautious encomiasts have ventured to pronounce it, and that the language of conventional panegyric may even fall short of the unvarnished truth' (p. 29).

Roman law should be studied, he argued, because the world was getting smaller and ultimately the legal methods of most advanced systems of law would be close to those developed by the civil law systems. They were technically ahead of us and we should recognise that fact.

> It is not because our own jurisprudence and that of Rome were *once* alike that they ought to be studied together, – it is because they *will be* alike. It is because all laws, however dissimilar in their infancy, tend to resemble each other in their maturity; and because we in England are slowly, and perhaps unconsciously or unwillingly, but still steadily and certainly accustoming ourselves to the same modes of legal thought and to the same conceptions of legal principle to which

---

[20] *Practical Jurisprudence: a comment on Austin* (Cambridge, 1883), 4–5.
[21] *Remains of R. H. Froude* (London, 1838), 1.310.
[22] 'Roman Law and Legal Education', *Cambridge Essays* (London, 1856), 1–29; reprinted in *Village Communities in East and West*, 7th edn (London, 1895), 330–83.

the Roman jurisconsults had attained after centuries of accumulated experience and unwearied cultivation (p. 2).

'However dissimilar in their infancy': when he wrote those words, Maine was already preparing the lectures which became *Ancient Law*, whose significant subtitle was: *its connection with the early history of society and its relation to modern ideas.*[23] It was an attempt to expound the historical development of the legal conceptions which were incorporated into the social system of his own time, such as property, disposition by will, contract, crime and punishment. In the preface he explains that there could have been no hope of prosecuting the inquiry, 'if there had not existed a body of law, like that of the Romans, bearing in its earliest portions the traces of the most remote antiquity, and supplying from its later rules the staple of the civil institutions by which modern society is even now controlled. The necessity of taking Roman law as a typical system' made him draw most of his illustrations from that system. Although Maine expressly disavowed his intention to write a treatise on Roman jurisprudence, he was certainly conscious of the need, felt by all British teachers of Roman law, to insist on the importance of their subject and to demonstrate to their students its relevance to an understanding of institutions in English law.

Maine saw himself as a fighter against pure abstractions and *a priori* assumptions, such as the state of nature and the law of nature. Speculations about man in the first ages of the world were useless, in his view, because they were made 'by first supposing mankind to be divested of a great part of the circumstances by which they are now surrounded, and by then assuming that, in the condition thus imagined, they would preserve the same sentiments and prejudices by which they are now actuated – although in fact these sentiments may have been created and engendered by those very circumstances of which, by the hypothesis, they are to be stripped' (ch. VIII,, pp. 149–50). By contrast, he saw his own work as scientific, empirical and inductive.

In an address to the students at Calcutta University in the mid-1860s, he told his 'native auditors':

It is now affirmed, and was felt long before it was affirmed, that the truth of history, if it exists, cannot differ from any other form of truth. If it be truth at

[23] Page references in the text are to the Everyman's Library edition of *Ancient Law*, 1972 reprint.

all it must be scientific truth. There can be no essential difference between the truths of the Astronomer, of the Physiologist, and of the Historian. The great principle which underlies all our knowledge of the physical world, that Nature is ever consistent with herself, must also be true of human nature and human society which is made up of human nature. It is not, indeed, meant that there are no truths except of the external world, but that all truth, of whatever character, must conform to the same conditions, so that, if indeed history be true, it must teach that which every other science teaches – continuous sequence, inflexible order, and eternal law (*Village Communities in the East and West*, 1895 edn, 265–6).

The science which provided the model for Maine was geology.[24] At the beginning of *Ancient Law*, he says of the rudimentary ideas of early law that they 'are to the jurist what the primary crusts of the earth are to the geologist. They contain, potentially, all the forms in which law has subsequently exhibited itself' (ch. 1, p. 2). Maine seems to refer to the uniformitarian doctrine, expounded by Sir Charles Lyell in his *Principles of Geology* in 1830. Lyell argued that changes in the earth's surface were not caused, as had been generally believed, by periodic but unpredictable sudden catastrophes but were rather the result of regular physical forces in constant, but gradual and almost imperceptible change.

This conception of the earth's structure provided an attractive analogy with the traditional view of the common law. From one point of view it was immemorial custom, presented as eternal and temporally indivisible, whereas from another it was gradually and imperceptibly being modified in countless individual decisions to fit new social conditions.

In early societies the law has potentially the forms of later law. As Maine put it later in Calcutta: 'Ancient history has for scientific purposes the great advantage over modern that it is incomparably simpler – simpler because younger. The actions of men, their motives and the movements of society are all infinitely less complex

---

[24] *Ancient Law* owed nothing to Darwin's *Origin of Species* (1859), although this is sometimes suggested, e.g. E. Patterson, *Jurisprudence: Men and ideas of the Law* (Brooklyn, 1953), 415, and P. Stein and J. Shand, *Legal Values in Western Society* (Edinburgh, 1974), 15 (*mea culpa*). G. Feaver, *From Status to Contract*, 1969, 41–2, points out that the first drafts of the book were written between 1855 and 1860, the final manuscript was completed by July 1860 and publication was in January, 1861. Discussing the influence of morality on crime in chapter IX, Maine says, 'At the moment at which I write, the newest chapter in the English criminal law is one which attempts to prescribe punishment for the frauds of trustees.' This must refer to 20 & 21 Vict., c. 54, which became law in August 1857.

than in the modern world, and better fitted therefore, to serve as materials for a first generalization' (*Village Communities*, 269).

To some extent Maine's insistence on being a scientific historian of legal ideas was the fashion of the time. He was concerned with scientific truth in the positivist manner of Comte and Grote. He was also concerned with the history of legal institutions in the manner of Savigny, whose influence on him is clear.[25] Just as Savigny combatted the view that law consists of the statutes of the legislator guided by natural law, so Maine rejected the view that it was the command of a legislator motivated by utilitarian principles. For 'the farther we penetrate into the primitive history of thought, the farther we find ourselves from a conception of law which at all resembles a compound of the elements which Bentham determined' (ch. I, pp. 4–5).

And again, more tortuously, on the process of legal change,

Bentham suggests the answer that societies modify, and have always modified, their laws according to modifications of their views of general expediency. It is difficult to say that this proposition is false, but it certainly appears to be unfruitful. For that which seems expedient to a society, or rather to the governing part of it, when it alters a rule of law, is surely the same thing as the object, whatever it may be, which it has in view when it makes the change. Expediency and the greatest good are nothing more than different names for the impulse which prompts the modification; and when we lay down expediency as the rule of change in law or opinion, all we get by the proposition is the substitution of an express term for a term which is necessarily implied when we say that a change takes place (ch. V, p. 70).

To counteract Benthamism, Maine, like Savigny, turned to history. We have noted that earlier legal writers had categorised Savigny in the same class as Comte, because they both offered an apparently similar historical account of legal development, and here we must be careful of our terms. Comte called his scientific philosophy 'positive' and his followers called themselves positivists. For lawyers, however, positivist has a more technical connotation,

---

[25] Sir F. Pollock, *Introduction and Notes to Sir Henry Maine's Ancient Law*, 2nd edn (London, 1908), x: 'In Roman law Savigny, then still living, was the person of greatest authority.' C. K. Allen, Introduction to World's Classics edn (Oxford, 1954), xiii, suggested that Maine was influenced by Jhering. There are similarities in their work, but the *Geist des Römischen Rechts* did not obviously influence *Ancient Law*, and (in regard to influence of Maine) Jhering told Pollock that he did not easily read English (Pollock, *ibid.*); cf. Burrow, *Evolution*, 142.

namely, one who, like Bentham, holds that all law is positive, laid down by an authoritative legislator. Comte's positivism was opposed to legal positivism in this sense.

Maine no doubt felt that he was more scientific and less romantic than Savigny, but they shared a similar pre-occupation with 'progressive' (Maine) or 'nobler' (Savigny) nations, of which the Romans were the model; they agreed on the importance of the Roman juristic method for an understanding of the mechanisms of legal change, and they were at one in their emphasis on continuity of national traditions. Maine criticises Montesquieu for considering

> the nature of man as entirely plastic, as passively reproducing the impressions, and submitting implicitly to the impulses, which it receives from without. And here no doubt lies the error which vitiates his system as a system. He greatly underrates the stability of human nature. He pays little or no regard to the inherited qualities of the race, those qualities which each generation receives from its predecessors and transmits but slightly altered to the generation which follows it (ch. v, pp. 68–9).

Maine wrote *Ancient Law* at a time when there was a new interest in the social institutions as distinct from the events of antiquity. The standard counterpart for Rome to Grote's *History of Greece* was the English translation of B. G. Niebuhr's great *Römische Geschichte*. This was an earlier work, which first appeared in the original German in 1811, and it was criticised by Grote for being too conjectural. Yet Niebuhr distinguished between different kinds of source material and used legends as evidence of the conditions in a particular stage in a society's development. He compared societies which were similar in structure though separated from each other in time and place. He was an admirer of Savigny,[26] and there is a romantic touch in the parallel which he drew between early Roman society and the agrarian society of North Friesland where he had grown up.

Discussing tribes or 'houses', he remarked, 'If anyone makes the presumptuous attempt to frame a distinct conception of the way in which states arose out of a foregoing order of things where no civil society existed, he is forced to mount up in thought to an age when such families as spring from one stock live united in a

[26] Preface to 2nd edn, dated December 1826.

patriarchal manner into a little community.' The philosophers of the Lyceum succumbed to this illusion. 'Their mistake lay only in confounding the systematical institutions enacted by legislation, with such as were the growth of nature, the prototypes which suggested those institutions. For had there not been the example of houses that had grown out of families, no-one would have formed any as the elements of states.'[27]

This 'semi-conjectural' approach struck a sympathetic chord in Maine.

> Whether we look to the Greek states, or to Rome, or to the Teutonic aristocracies in Ditmarsh, which furnished Niebuhr with so many valuable illustrations, or to the Celtic clan associations, or to that strange social organisation of the Sclavonic Russians and Poles which has only lately attracted notice, everywhere we discover traces of passages in their history when men of alien descent were admitted to, and amalgamated with, the original brotherhood (ch. v, p. 76).

Passages like this suggest that, despite his energetic claims to be scientific, Maine's methods were in fact closer to Niebuhr's more impressionistic approach than they were to Grote's. Maine had an exact knowledge of Roman law and its history but he avoided giving precise details of non-Roman institutions, and his references to them often appear to be little more than illustrations of Roman institutions in the Niebuhr manner.

The passage just cited also shows another characteristic of Maine's *Ancient Law*, namely its limitation to Indo-European, or Aryan peoples. Maine claimed to be not only historical but also comparative, but his comparisons were limited. This concentration seems to have been the result of the contemporary interest in comparative philology. Hume had recognised, and Savigny had stressed, the affinity between law and language in the manner of their development. The implications of comparative philology for evolutionary theory of language were explained by its leading exponent in England, Max Müller, in a review of the English translation of Bopp's *Comparative Grammar* in the *Edinburgh Review* in 1851.

Philology's first task, he announced, was to collect a mass of material about different languages. It then

[27] *History of Rome*, translated by J. C. Hare and C. Thirlwall, 2nd edn, vol. 1 (Cambridge, 1831), 304–5.

uses the literary remains of all nations as a means to arrive at an understanding of the nature and laws of language. Language itself becomes the object of inquiry...if we observe the great changes which each of these languages has undergone in the course of centuries, we see that language has, like man, a history of its own...It is clear, therefore, that the nature of language cannot be studied either in the abstract or by means of but one of its numerous varieties, like our own language, but that an historical method alone can lead to satisfactory results (XCIV.299–300).

Languages must be classified into groups 'according to the peculiar character of their etymological and grammatical structure' (p. 305). The only group seriously studied so far is that comprising 'the languages of the Indo-European or Arian family' (p. 310). 'As soon as Sanskrit appeared above the horizon, the broad fact of the connexion of the Arian languages became as clear as daylight', but the establishment of connection is only a first step to 'penetrating into the secrets of lingual development' (p. 317). More than that, it enables us 'to reconstruct on a firmer basis the oldest history of the whole Arian family' (p. 328).

Following this lead, Maine paid no attention to the legal customs of savage tribes, such as the American Indians. He worked almost exclusively from written sources, and his account is essentially limited to Roman and, to a lesser extent, English law, with occasional references to Greek and Indian materials. Although Maine's detailed study of Indian law was the product of his service in India, after the publication of *Ancient Law*, he showed already in that work an acquaintance with the Hindu Code of Manu (or Menu, as he called it). It was not difficult to obtain some idea of it. In 1796, Sir William Jones had published an English translation of *The Institutes of Hindu Law or the Ordinances of Menu*, and both Sanskrit and English versions were published with a preface by Jones in 1825. The Burmese version, with English translation, was published in 1847.

What does surprise us, in view of Maine's concentration on Indo-European materials, is the fact that *Ancient Law* contains direct references neither to the Anglo-Saxon laws, of which the Record Commission had published an elaborate edition, with translation, in 1840, nor the ancient laws of Wales, which the Commission had published, with translation, in 1841. For Anglo-Saxon institutions, he relied on J. M. Kemble's *The Saxons in England* (2 vols., London, 1849).

Maine began his account of *Ancient Law* with the earliest forms of law recorded in writing, which he called Ancient Codes, exemplified by the Twelve Tables in Rome, the Code of Solon at Athens and the laws of Menu in India. He argued that they were not legislation in the modern sense but rather authoritative records of what was established custom. They were the first public statement to everybody in the community 'as to what he was to do, and what not to do' (ch. 1, p. 9).

Before their appearance, there was first an early stage when even custom did not exist. Men's lives were controlled by arbitrary decisions handed down by the patriarch or king. These were the *themistes* of the Homeric poems, which purported to be divinely inspired, and were not laws, but judgements. 'They cannot be supposed to be connected by any thread of principle; they are separate, isolated judgements' (ch. 1, p. 3).

Subsequently, as in the passage from Monarchy to Republic in early Rome, the divinely inspired kings lost their sacred power and were replaced by small groups of aristocrats. They claimed to be the repositories of the traditional customary rules by which disputes were settled. This was 'the epoch of customary law'. At first customs could be preserved only by confiding them to a privileged caste. Then, 'the aristocracies seem to have abused their monopoly of legal knowledge; and at all events their exclusive possession of the law was a formidable impediment to the success of those popular movements which began to be universal in the western world' (ch. 1, p. 9).

The next stage is that of the ancient codes, which are usually the result of popular agitation and follow the discovery of writing. By removing the custody of the law from the aristocrats, and freezing the statement of the customs into a fixed form of words, the codes end the spontaneous growth of law. Subsequent legal development is the product of deliberate effort to adapt the law stated in the codes to changes in the conditions of society.

At this point Maine introduces the distinction between stationary societies and progressive societies. The latter are the exception in the world, since man is innately conservative. 'Much the greatest part of mankind has never shown a particle of desire that its civil institutions should be improved since the moment when external completeness was first given to them by their embodiment in some permanent record' (ch. I, p. 14). The typical stationary society is the Hindu, which failed to develop its law after the publication of the laws of Menu. Maine was concerned only with progressive societies, and conveniently, 'nothing is more remarkable than their extreme fewness' (ch. I, p. 13). The typical progressive societies are, of course, the Roman and the English. In such societies the archaic law laid down in the ancient codes (Maine omitted to indicate what he regarded as the equivalent of an ancient code for England) was modified by three successive instruments of legal change: first fictions, then equity and finally legislation.

Fiction is the most primitive of these and makes legal change possible at a time when it cannot be admitted openly that the law is being changed. It is an assumption for legal purposes that something is the case which everyone knows is not the case. So it conceals or affects to conceal the fact that the law has been altered. The law is formally unchanged but it now includes a new class within its scope. When one who is not a father's child is considered to be his child for legal purposes, by adoption, that is a fiction. There are fictions in the pontifical interpretation of the Roman Twelve Tables, and in the efforts of the medieval English courts to increase their jurisdiction by pretending that classes of cases, which they had not previously dealt with, were really within their jurisdiction.

Equity involves recourse to 'a set of legal principles, entitled by their intrinsic superiority to supersede the older law' (ch. III, p. 26). These principles are assumed to have universal validity, and exist alongside the pre-existing strict civil law, which they eventually supersede. Equity is always introduced by a magistrate. The praetor in Rome and the Chancellor in England provided the means of introducing equity into their respective systems.

The last of the ameliorating instrumentalities is legislation, open law-making. It differs from the others because it derives its authority and obligatory force from an external body or person, not from a set of principles. Maine took the opportunity to make a dig at Bentham. 'It is the more necessary to note these differences, because a student of Bentham would be apt to confound Fictions, Equity and Statute Law under the single head of legislation. They all, he would say, involve *law-making*' (ch. II, p. 18).

Observing that an adequate discussion of English equity required a separate treatise, Maine then gives a detailed account of Roman equity, bringing out that the moral principles which the praetor introduced into Roman law were derived from Greek ideas of nature and natural law. They became Romanised through 'the alliance of the lawyers with the Stoic philosophers' (ch. III, p. 32). He concludes with two general points. One is that equity tends in time to become as strict as the law which it has modified. 'A time always comes at which the moral principles originally adopted have been carried out to all their legitimate consequences, and then the system founded on them becomes as rigid, as unexpansive, and as liable to fall behind moral progress as the sternest code of rules avowedly legal' (ch. III, p. 40). This point was reached in Rome in the reign of Alexander Severus, and in England in the Chancellorship of Lord Eldon, who explained and harmonised English equity instead of enlarging it. Maine underlines the inevitable nature of this process. 'If the philosophy of legal history were better understood in England, Lord Eldon's services would be less exaggerated on the one hand and better appreciated on the other' (*ibid.*).

The other characteristic of both English and Roman equity is the 'falsehood of the assumptions upon which the claim of the equitable to superiority over the legal rule is originally defended' (ch. III, p. 41). Instead of being presented as a morally superior rule, it is explained as the recovery of an ancient rule. In Rome equity was justified as the rule of a natural state before the advent of civil society; in England it was referred to the idea that the king superintends the administration of justice, and that it flowed from the king's conscience.

After a somewhat tendentious account of 'the modern history of the law of nature', Maine arrives in chapter v at 'Primitive Society and Ancient Law' itself. Early society, he shows, begins not with the individual but with the family group, and the remainder of the book consists of a series of confirmatory examples of this proposition. The early history of wills, property, contract and delict, and crime are all explained by reference to his theory of the primitive family.

In early societies relations between the members are controlled by status, 'a condition of society in which all the relations of

Persons are summed up in the relations of Family' (ch. v, p. 99). The primitive family or kinship group is dominated by the patriarch; this part is pure Roman law. The members are subjected to the power of the *paterfamilias*. 'In truth, in the primitive view, Relationship is exactly limited by Patria Potestas. Where the Potestas begins, Kinship begins' (ch. v, p. 88). Strangers are absorbed into the family by adoption, and we must

> regard the fiction of adoption as so closely simulating the reality of kinship that neither law nor opinion makes the slightest difference between a real and an adoptive connexion...The persons theoretically amalgamated into a family by their common descent are practically held together by common obedience to their highest living ascendant, the father, grandfather or great-grandfather. The patriarchal authority of a chieftain is as necessary an ingredient in the notion of the family group as the fact (or assumed fact) of its having sprung from his loins (ch. v, pp. 78-9).

The descendants of females, being in the power of another patriarch, are therefore 'outside the limits of archaic kinship' (ch. v, p. 88).

At this point Maine strains to the limit his practice of generalising the particular experience of Roman law.

> We have in the annals of Roman law a nearly complete history of the crumbling away of an archaic system, and of the formation of new institutions from the recombined materials, institutions some of which descended unimpaired to the modern world, while others, destroyed or corrupted by contact with barbarism in the dark ages, had again to be recovered by mankind...
>
> The movement of progressive societies has been uniform in one respect. Through all its course it has been distinguished by the gradual dissolution of family dependency and the growth of individual obligation in its place. The Individual is steadily substituted for the Family, as the unit of which civil laws take account. The advance has been accomplished at varying rates of celerity...But, whatever its pace, the change has not been subject to reaction or recoil, and apparent retardations will be found to have been occasioned by the absorption of archaic ideas and customs from some entirely foreign source...The tie between man and man which replaces by degrees those forms of reciprocity in rights and duties which have their origin in the Family...is Contract...We seem to have steadily moved towards a phase of social order in which all these relations arise from the free agreement of Individuals.

He goes on to show how the status of the slave, the status of the female under tutelage, the status of a son under power have all disappeared.

The climax of the argument is reached with Maine's most

famous generalisation. If we use the word status to signify 'these personal conditions only and avoid applying the term to such conditions as are the immediate or remote result of agreement, we may say that the movement of progressive societies has hitherto been a movement from *Status to Contract*' (ch. v, pp. 98–100).

The force and style of this passage explain in part why *Ancient Law* made such a tremendous impact on publication. The authoritative ease and fluency with which Maine formulated his ideas carried great conviction. He presented his findings as axiomatic propositions, which had only to be stated to be immediately accepted. One of the features of *Ancient Law* was the absence of references to sources. Unlike the traditional antiquarian treatise, it was not loaded with footnotes. A reviewer in the *Law Magazine and Review* wrote in the year of its publication:

> Not the least of the characteristics of this book is its apparent simplicity. As the author has, wisely as we think, forborne to encumber his pages with citation of authorities, they do not at a first glance suggest that accumulation of learning which is apt to repel the general reader. But even the most flowing and brilliant passages are in many cases charged with much condensed thought and research. Mr Maine evidently does not write for lawyers only (N.S. XI.124).

The style of *Ancient Law* was an important part of its enormous influence. So also was its object. The same reviewer announced,

> We have no hesitation in saying that nothing resembling it has yet appeared in an English dress...Scarcely any attempt...has...yet been made – at least in this country – to expound the historical affiliation of those legal conceptions which are incorporated into the very life and movement of our existing social system...The scope of the book is nothing less than a historical deduction of elementary legal conceptions from the earliest ages of which we have any written record. It tracks these legal conceptions to their cradle (N.S. XI.99–100).

Some observers considered Maine's approach to jurisprudence not as opposed to that of Bentham and Austin but as complementary to it. Noting that Maine had in fact used some of Austin's findings, they saw that whereas the earlier writers had based their abstractions on the present state of the law in an advanced society, Maine was extending the method of inductive generalisation to historical data, and not merely to Roman law, as Savigny had done. 'We have arrived at a point when it is both necessary and possible to embrace in the induction legal systems far more remote from us than the Roman, both in time, in geographical position, and in the strangeness of the ideas to which they introduce us.'[28] Other sciences had their natural history. Now at last, as Pollock put it, we had 'the natural history of law'. Maine

> showed, on the one hand, that legal ideas and institutions have a real course of development as much as the genera and species of living creatures... on the other hand, he made it clear that these processes deserve and require distinct study, and cannot be treated as mere incidents in the general history of the societies where they occur... Maine has taught us... that law has an important history of its own, not at all confined to its political and constitutional aspects.[29]

We have noticed that some of his individual points had been made by earlier writers. Long had drawn attention to the importance of fictions. Grote analysed the nature of *themistes*. McLennan saw the significance of contract in relation to status. Some of Maine's specific results, such as the relationship of testamentary succession to family structure, which he claimed to be the best demonstration of 'the superiority of the historical method of investigation to the modes of inquiry concerning Jurisprudence which are in fashion among us' (ch. VI, p. 101), had been at least partially anticipated by the Scottish thinkers of the previous century. But if not all the ideas discussed by Maine were original, he made them his own by weaving them into a coherent fabric.

So many of Maine's *aperçus* have become commonplaces of legal thought that we tend to forget their origin. Examples readily occur: the religious awe evoked by law in early societies; the strict formalism of archaic law; the predominance of procedural over substantive rules in early law (as he said in a later work, 'substantive law has at first the look of being gradually secreted in the interstices of procedure'),[30] the relatively late appearance of the individual's power of testamentary disposition, of freedom of contract and of public criminal law as opposed to reparation for the victim of crime.

It was Maine's apparently intuitive genius for generalisation that converted such ideas into the common currency of legal thought.

---

[28] *Law Magazine and Review*, N.S. XI (1861), 236 (review of Austin's *The Province of Jurisprudence Determined*).
[29] *Introduction and Notes*, viii.
[30] *Early Law and Custom* (London, 1891), 389.

5

The aftermath of *Ancient Law*

With the publication of *Ancient Law*, legal evolution reached its zenith. The mid-Victorians welcomed the doctrine that the law of civilised societies was the product of a development through a series of identifiable stages related to, but distinct from, the development of society itself. Legal evolution can be regarded as a species of the theories of social evolution which became popular in the 1850s and 1860s. They were attractive to Victorians who were conscious, and a little apprehensive, despite optimistic assertions of confidence, of the great social changes taking place around them, and who were ready to embrace theories that ascribed these changes to inevitable impersonal laws. Such theories

> offered a way of reformulating the essential unity of mankind, while avoiding the current objections to the older theories of a human nature everywhere essentially the same. Mankind was one not because it was everywhere the same, but because the differences represented different stages in the same process. And by agreeing to call the process progress, one could convert the social theory into a moral and political one.[1]

Maine's *Ancient Law* was re-assuring to those who were becoming numbed by the spate of Benthamite law reforms. The historian Charles Merivale wrote of the revelation which Maine's account of Roman law gave of 'a revolution of one thousand years of constant progress, without a violent shock throughout'.[2] The success of *Ancient Law* owes much to its superb literary form; but it also exactly fitted the mood of the times. In particular, it tied in with general intellectual movements which were in the air.

First, the popularity of determinist history was associated with the prestige of science, in the narrow British sense of natural

[1] J. W. Burrow, *Evolution and Society* (Cambridge, 1966), 98–9.
[2] *Autobiography and Letters of Charles Merivale*, ed. J. A. Merivale (London, 1898), 321, cited by G. Feaver, *From Status to Contract* (London, 1969), 274.

science. It was characterised by the quest for what Maine called 'external law', in the sense of simple explanations for a complex series of observations. The methods of the physical sciences could be applied to society and its institutions because all sorts of facts about social institutions were now available for the first time. New collections of statistics were making people aware of regularities in man's behaviour, which had not previously been dreamed of. Murder is the most unpredictable of men's acts, yet in the mid-nineteenth century it was discovered that murder is committed, as H. T. Buckle saw it, 'with as much regularity, and bears as uniform a relation to certain known circumstances, as do the movements of the tides and the rotations of the seasons'. If it could be shown that men's good and bad actions vary according to the changes in the surrounding society, then 'we shall be forced to the further conclusion that such variations are the result of large and general causes, which, working upon the aggregate of society, must produce certain consequences, without regard to the volition of those particular men of whom the society is composed'.[3]

Secondly, legal evolution fitted into the vogue for thinking in terms of biological evolution, which followed the publication of Darwin's *Origin of Species* in 1859. *Ancient Law* was probably substantially completed before then, and shows geological rather than biological influences, but after its publication, readers readily saw a similarity between the evolution of the organisms which were animal and the evolution of the organisms which constituted societies. Maine himself accepted this parallel. In a later work, when discussing the motives which impel man to the labour and pain which produce wealth in ever-increasing quantities, he wrote: 'They are the springs of action called into activity by the strenuous and never-ending struggle for existence, the beneficent private war which makes one man strive to climb on the shoulders of another and remain there through the law of the survival of the fittest.'[4]

Further, as he admitted frankly in a minute to the Government of India, 'even jurisprudence itself cannot escape from the great law of evolution'.[5]

[3] *History of Civilization* (2 vols., London, 1857–61), I.21–3.
[4] *Popular Government*, 5th edn (London, 1897), 50.
[5] Appendix to Minute to Government of India, cited by M. E. Grant Duff, *Sir Henry Maine* (London, 1892), 60; cf. P. J. Bowler, 'The changing meaning of "evolution"', *Journal of History of Ideas*, 36 (1975), 102ff.

Even those who were unimpressed by this kind of science were not disappointed by *Ancient Law*, for there was a distinctly idealistic strain in the work. There were those, like Hegel, who taught that the historian should not be satisfied with collecting facts and arranging them in sequences, but must seek the meaning and point of the whole historical process. For Hegel this was to be found in the idea of freedom. The history of the world demonstrates the emergence of the consciousness of freedom and then of its realisation, assisted by the forces of continuity and hindered by those of inertia.[6] Maine had demonstrated the movement of progressive societies, which he stressed were the exception rather than the rule, from status to contract. Those who saw history as the gradual attainment of an ideal like freedom recognised in his exposition the gradual unfolding of the idea of the self-determination of the free individual, projected on the plane of law.

These currents of opinion ensured the success of legal evolution in the elegant form in which Maine had dressed it. The brilliance and authoritative air of his generalisations were then, and remain today, very persuasive. It was not long, however, before objections began to appear. They came from various quarters. Some were from professional scholars, who complained that some of Maine's conclusions were just not supported by the evidence. Others were directed more to the methodological basis of his theories, and others again to their political implications. These objections must now be considered.

First, scholars specialising in the social institutions of primitive man — the protagonists of the anthropology which was just emerging as a separate discipline — argued that the facts on which Maine's propositions were apparently based were in some cases wrong and in any case did not justify the general character that he claimed for them. For all his pretensions to have traced 'the real, as opposed to the imaginary, or the arbitrarily assumed, history of the institutions of civilized man' (*Early Law and Custom*, 1891 edn, p. 192), they suggested that his generalisations should be treated as nothing more than merely provisional hypotheses.

In the same year that *Ancient Law* was published, J. J. Bachofen, a Swiss pupil of Savigny, who had been Professor of Roman Law

[6] W. H. Walsh, *An Introduction to the Philosophy of History*, 3rd edn (London, 1967), 139–43.

at Basel but resigned to devote himself to art history, published *Das Mutterrecht*; four years later J. F. McLennan, the author of the unorthodox *Britannica* article on Law, published *Primitive Marriage: an Inquiry into the Origin of the Form of Capture in Marriage Ceremonies*; and in 1871 L. H. Morgan, the American ethnologist, published his *Systems of Consanguinity and Affinity of the Human Family*. The common feature of all these works was that they set out a theory of the origin of the family which was precisely the opposite of Maine's. Though they did not realise it, their authors were developing an idea adumbrated by John Millar. For patriarchy they substituted matriarchy. At first, they held, individual marriage was unknown. Promiscuity and resulting uncertain paternity prevailed. Children were regarded as belonging to the group as a whole rather than as the offspring of a particular family. It was the mother who was important rather than the father. Hence descent is matrilineal and mother-right prevails.

Maine rejected the new views with vigour. Although in *Ancient Law* he had not studied periods earlier than the evidence of written records allowed, now that his pride was stung he offered views of primitive family life which were not based on evidence at all but on a projection backwards of the known structure of the early Roman family, on which he had based his patriarchal theory. In *Early Law and Custom* he wrote:

> The strongest and wisest male rules. He jealously guards his wife or wives. All under his protection are on an equality. The strange child who is taken under it, the stranger who is brought under it to serve, are not distinguished from the child born under the shelter. But when wife, child, or slave escapes, there is an end to all relations with the group, and the kinship which means submission to power or participation in protection is at an end. This is the family (to borrow Sir George Cox's energetic expression) of the wild beast in his den (p. 198).

As Professor Robson comments, 'I think it may safely be said that no such savage family ever was on land or sea. The whole construction is a piece of pure *histoire raisonée*.'[7]

The controversy over matriarchy or patriarchy was only the first which was raised by anthropologists in regard to Maine's ideas. Of course, we must remember that, when Maine wrote, anthropological investigation was in its infancy. Since his time field work

[7] W. A. Robson, 'Sir Henry Maine today', *Modern Theories of Law* (London, 1933), 167.

among non-Indo-European tribes, particularly in Africa, North America and the Pacific Islands, has produced a picture of primitive life far different from that envisaged by Maine. Furthermore, anthropologists have concentrated their attention on societies which are still at a pre-literate stage. Maine, on the other hand, was primarily concerned with the period when early law begins to be recorded in writing, and, in *Ancient Law* at least, he tended to regard his schemes of legal development as valid for Indo-European or Aryan societies only. Although he sometimes did not resist the temptation to extrapolate backwards in time, and to generalise in a universal way, he was less concerned with pre-literate societies and with non-Aryan societies.

Modern anthropology has modified Maine's ideas on two general features which he ascribed to early law. In the first place, he has been shown to have underestimated the place of magic and superstition in early law. Maine had observed that law and religion were often indistinguishable, and that the earliest exponents of legal customs were also priests of the state religious cult. 'There is no system of recorded law, literally from China to Peru, which, when it first emerges into notice, is not seen to be entangled with religious ritual and observance' (*Early Law and Custom*, p. 5).

He assumed that when law and religion are separated from each other the supernatural element in law disappears. More recent research has shown, however, that when society's machinery for directly enforcing the law is insufficiently strong, it may use magic to enforce a legal judgement.[8] The supernatural consequences of taboo, the practice of enforced suicide, and other typical features of the anthropological picture of primitive law enforcement, have no place in Maine's scheme. This is partly because magic was not prominent in Roman law, when it was first recorded. Since Maine's day, we have learned that magic survived longer, even among the Romans, than was thought possible by rational Victorians.[9]

Another feature which Maine derived from Roman law and which anthropologists have found difficult to accept is his stress

---

[8] E. A. Hoebel, *The Law of Primitive Man* (Cambridge, Mass., 1954), 257ff.
[9] G. MacCormack, 'Formalism, Symbolism and Magic in early Roman Law', *Tijdschrift voor Rechtsgeschiedenis*, 37 (1969), 439–68, and 'Haegerstroem's Magical Interpretation of Roman Law', *Irish Jurist*, 4 (1969), 153–67.

on the stiff and ritualistic character of early law, once it has been formulated. He spoke of 'the rigidity of primitive law, arising from its early association and identification with religion, [which] has chained down the mass of the human race to those views of life and conduct which they entertained at the time when their usages were first consolidated into a systematic form'. Apart from one or two exceptions, 'it is still true that over the larger part of the world, the perfection of law has always been considered as consisting in adherence to the ground plan supposed to have been marked out by the original legislator' (*Ancient Law*, ch. IV, pp. 45–6). E. A. Hoebel comments, 'If ever Sir Henry Maine fixed an erroneous notion on modern legal historians, it was the idea that primitive law, once formulated, is stiff and ritualistic (and by implication weak in juristic method)' (p. 283).

In this respect I believe that there has been misunderstanding of Maine's view, due perhaps to some unguarded language. Maine was concerned with the difficulty of developing law at a time when writing had been discovered and there was a popular demand for legal custom to be removed from the custody of a small clique and made available generally in a public document. That was the origin of primitive codes, and wherever they were found, there was a tendency to treat their texts as sacrosanct. Most primitive societies studied by anthropologists do not have written codes. They are at the pre-code stage of customary law, so that the problem of formalism would not in Maine's view arise.

The main result of anthropological research is that any scheme of universal legal evolution must be rejected. Such is the variety found in different societies at the same stage of social and economic development that we must hold with Hoebel that 'there has been no straight line of development in the growth of law' (p. 288). There is no automatic connection between a particular level of cultural development and particular legal techniques or legal ideas. One reason for the variety is due to the borrowing of legal notions by one society from another at a different stage of development, a phenomenon not considered by Maine. But if there is no single line of development, what of the particular trends which Maine identified as characteristics of early law?

In recent years there has been a debate between anthropologists on the extent to which the analyses of historical jurisprudence based on Western (i.e. Roman and Germanic) law may properly be used to explain the laws of simpler non-European societies. Professor P. J. Bohannan has stressed the difficulties of translating a legal concept from one culture to another and insists on the uniqueness of the laws of different societies, each of which has to be considered in its own terms.[10] Professor Max Gluckman, on the other hand, held that the central concepts of law – obligation, guilt and innocence, tort, crime, contract and so on – are found in most legal systems, even those of undeveloped societies, although their attributes may vary in detail. In regard to such specific legal relationships, many of the ideas put forward by Maine are still generally applicable at some point in the development of most legal systems, although it may not be possible to keep the evolutionary scheme in which he set them.

In the preface to his *Ideas in Barotse Jurisprudence*,[11] Gluckman argued that 'once we recognize that he was in fact analysing relatively advanced types of legal systems', modern anthropological research in general 'validates the chief outlines of Maine's analysis'. He even suggested that a more accurate title for his book would have been 'Footnotes to Sir Henry Maine's *Ancient Law*' (p. xvi). Among Maine's ideas which Gluckman found helpful to explain Barotse jurisprudence was his contention that 'the separation of the Law of Persons from that of Things has no meaning in the infancy of law', the rules being 'inextricably mingled together' (ch. VIII, p. 152; Gluckman, 94). We cannot describe landholding, except in terms of the personal status of the owner, nor can the status of a person be divorced from his rights to land. Again, Maine's observation that in early law, 'conveyances and contracts were practically confounded' (ch. IX, p. 186), and that 'a contract was long regarded as an incomplete conveyance' (ch. IX, p. 189), is confirmed by the Barotse law of sale (Gluckman, 183–4). A further helpful notion is Maine's explanation of Roman succession on death as being not a succession to specific items of property but rather to a *universitas juris*, 'a collection of rights and duties united

---

[10] *Justice and Judgement among the Tiv of Central Nigeria* (London, 1957).
[11] (New Haven, Conn., 1965), xvi; cf. Gluckman, 'African Traditional Law in Historical Perspective', *Proceedings British Academy*, 60 (1974), 295–337.

by the single circumstance of their having belonged at one time to some one person. It is, as it were, the legal clothing of some given individual' (ch. VI, p. 105; Gluckman, 124).

So rich is the material in *Ancient Law* that even if we must jettison some of it, there is much of value left in its more specific observations, which have created type-situations that we look out for in approaching an unfamiliar legal system.[12]

The second line of attack was mounted by legal historians, and especially English legal historians, who felt that whether or not Maine's ideas applied to Roman law or Hindu law, they should at least be applicable to early English law and its Germanic antecedents. Frederick William Maitland, the greatest of all English legal historians, was critical of Maine's assumptions and his rather cavalier way with the original sources. As he wrote to his collaborator Pollock, an admirer of Maine:

> You spoke of Maine. Well, I always talk of him with reluctance, for on the few occasions on which I sought to verify his statements of fact I came to the conclusion that he trusted much to a memory that played him tricks and rarely looked at a book that he had once read: e.g. his story about the position of the half-blood in the Law of Normandy seems to me a mere dream that is contradicted by every version of the custumal.[13]

To be sure, Maine's interest was not in detailed legal history, but in establishing general principles of development in early law. However, Maitland found that some of Maine's most famous and oft-quoted theses were not justified when applied to early Germanic law. The patriarchal theory and the village community theory will serve as examples.

A central thesis of *Ancient Law* was that early society begins with the group, in particular the family, and that early law is concerned not with the individual but with the family. For legal purposes the family is represented by its head, whose patriarchal power extends over all its members, wife, sons, daughters, and remoter issue, and they were only released from it by his death. This theory had the advantage of providing an explanation for several features of early

---

[12] For a survey favourable to Maine, R. Redfield, 'Maine's *Ancient Law* in the light of primitive societies', *Western Political Quarterly*, 3 (1950), 574–89.
[13] *The Letters of F. W. Maitland*, ed. C. H. S. Fifoot (London, 1965), 222. The reference is to *Ancient Law*, ch. V, p. 89.

Roman law, such as its preference for agnation, the tracing of descent exclusively through males, rather than cognation, ordinary blood relationship; and the practice of adopting a son from another family by a transfer, arranged by the two family heads, rather in the way a football player is transferred from one team to another today. This was a way of preserving the family against the extinction of male heirs, as indeed was the testament. The theory also explained the perpetual tutelage of women in early law. The course of Roman law further illustrated the gradual emancipation of the adult members of the family from the power of the father. The law began to recognise them as individuals, and their condition, instead of being determined by their status within the family, came to be negotiated by voluntary agreement, that is, by contract.

Again in regard to property, Maine denied that early law recognised individual ownership. In early Rome there was some evidence of a family ownership before the law recognised the ownership of the *paterfamilias*. But by that time Rome had already become a city state. For evidence of the earlier stage in the development of the law of property, Maine turned to the village communities of India, which he considered exemplified the expansion of the family into a larger group of co-owners, holding the village land in common. 'The Village Community of India is at once an organised patriarchal society and an assemblage of co-proprietors' (ch. VIII, p. 153), and 'the Russian Village appears to be a nearly exact repetition of the Indian Community' (p. 157), although there were differences in detail. In *Ancient Law*, Maine avoided any mention of Anglo-Saxon village communities, although Kemble, his source for the Anglo-Saxons, had found them in early England. Ten years later, after personal experience of Indian village communities during his service as Legal Member of the Viceroy's Council from 1862 to 1869, he returned to the subject in more detail in *Village Communities in the East and West*, and there he discussed the Germanic communities at some length. The work attracted much attention, and the topic was considered one of the pillars of its author's reputation as an historical jurist.[14]

[14] J. W. Burrow, '"The Village Community" and the Uses of History in Late Nineteenth-Century England', *Historical Perspectives*, ed. N. McKendrick (London, 1974), 255–84.

Maitland found that when he applied these theses to the earliest English law of which we have knowledge, he ran into difficulties: 'It has become a commonplace among English writers that the family rather than the individual was the "unit" of ancient law. That there is truth in this saying we are very far from denying – the bond of blood was once a strong and sacred bond – but we ought not to be content with terms so vague as "family" and "unit"....' The grouping of men and women into mutually exclusive clans 'seems to imply almost of necessity that kinship is transmitted either only by males or only by females'. Yet, 'so soon as we begin to get rules about inheritance and blood-feud, the dead man's kinsfolk, those who must bear the feud and may share the *wergild*, consist in part of persons related to him through his father and in part of persons related to him through his mother'. The same person can belong to different kinship groups. 'If the law were to treat the clan as an unit for any purpose whatever, this would surely be the purpose of *wer* and blood-feud', but it does not do so. Anglo-Saxon societies did not, therefore, consist of patriarchal clans, united by agnatic relationship.[15]

In describing the role of the family head, Maine had used modern legal terms to convey an impression of his functions. Maitland exploited all his powers of irony to ridicule Maine's alleged anachronisms:

Sir Henry Maine has said that 'the Family, in fact, was a Corporation'. But then he has also told us that 'the Patriarch, for we must not yet call him the Paterfamilias', was a 'trustee for his children and kindred', and 'in the eye of the law' represented the collective body. This patriarchal trustee, who represents a corporation, looks to me, I must confess, suspiciously modern. He may be a savage, but he is in full evening dress. At any rate he is an individual man; and, if he is treated as trustee and representative, there is law enough for individuals and to spare. If we speak, we must speak with words; if we think, we must think with thoughts. We are moderns and our words and thoughts can not but be modern. Perhaps, as Mr. Gilbert once suggested, it is too late for us to be early English. Every thought will be too sharp, every word will imply too many contrasts. We must, it is to be feared, use many words and qualify our every statement until we have almost contradicted it. The outcome will not be so graceful, so lucid, as Maine's Ancient Law.[16]

[15] F. Pollock and F. W. Maitland, *History of English Law*, 2nd edn (2 vols., London, 1909), II.240–2.
[16] *Township and Borough* (Cambridge, 1898), 21–2. The reference is to *Ancient Law*, ch. VI, p. 108.

As with the early family, so also with the village community and its communal ownership of land. Maitland asks whether, when one said that land was owned by communities before it was owned by individuals, one was really speaking about ownership at all. Surely the thought is not so much of proprietary rights in the sense of rights of disposal as of control over the way land was used. To talk of ownership was to fall into anachronism. When a community has progressed beyond the pastoral stage and has reached a certain level of agricultural development, it requires the notion of landownershp. Maitland shows that this very soon becomes ownership by individuals, and he pointed out that in the case of the Germanic peoples, they might well have picked up the idea of individual ownership from the Romans, thus disturbing the scheme of legal evolution:

If the anthropologist will concede to the historian that he need not start from communalism as from a necessary and primitive datum, a large room will be open for our guesses when we speculate about the doings of a race of barbarians who have come into contact with Roman ideas. Even had our anthropologists at their command materials that would justify them in prescribing a normal programme for the human race and in decreeing that every independent portion of mankind must, if it is to move at all, move through one fated series of stages which may be designated as Stage A, Stage B, Stage C and so forth, we still should have to face the fact that the rapidly progressive groups have been just those which have not been independent, which have not worked out their own salvation, but have appropriated alien ideas and have thus been enabled, for anything that we can tell, to leap from Stage A to Stage X without passing through any intermediate stages. Our Anglo-Saxon ancestors did not arrive at the alphabet, or at the Nicene Creed, by traversing a long series of 'stages'; they leapt to the one and to the other.

But in truth we are learning that the attempt to construct a normal programme for all portions of mankind is idle and unscientific.[17]

In one case, at least, we may be grateful to Maine for provoking a brilliant piece of corrective research by Maitland. One of Maine's lofty and authoritative statements of English legal history concerned Bracton, the thirteenth-century writer on the laws and customs of England. Maine wrote:

That an English writer of the time of Henry III should have been able to put off on his countrymen as a compendium of pure English law, a treatise of which the entire form and a third of the contents were directly borrowed from the Corpus Juris, and that he should have ventured on this experiment in a country where

[17] *Doomsday Book and Beyond* (Cambridge, 1897), 345.

the systematic study of Roman law was formally proscribed, will always be among the most hopeless enigmas in the history of jurisprudence (ch. IV, p. 48).

'This', said Maitland, 'is stupendous exaggeration'.[18] His refutation produced *Bracton and Azo*, the beginning of modern Bracton studies.

Such examples undermined the authority of Maine's principal propositions as universal truths. Maitland showed that Maine's schemes were too ambitious and were built on too narrow a base in fact. But he did not reject Maine's aims or the value of the comparative method, which Maitland himself used to considerable effect in regard to specific legal notions, such as the Corporation. Legal evolution was more complex and less amenable to neat schemes than it had appeared to be to Maine. Yet he had opened people's eyes to the existence of similarities in the legal institutions of the most differing societies. Indeed, one of the principal factors which distinguished Maine from Savigny and the German historical school was Maine's complete lack of nationalism. Thus while Germanists, such as von Gierke, insisted on the Germanic peculiarities of the mark-community (the German version of the village community), Maine used much the same materials to show 'the idea of a constantly recurring combination which is no more German in essence than it is Indian or Slavonic'.[19] This perhaps accounts for his great appeal to less nationalistic continental jurists.

Thirdly, there appeared methodological objectors to Maine's theory of legal evolution. In the eighteenth century Adam Smith had geared his theory of legal development to economic factors; the mode of subsistence of the society largely determined the kind of law it had. But although many of his basic ideas appeared in the *Wealth of Nations*, those concerned with legal evolution were not published in his lifetime. The nineteenth-century theories which we have considered, such as those of Savigny and Maine, were seen by contemporaries to be based more on the unfolding of certain ideas; the national spirit, the movement from status to contract. In the second half of the nineteenth century, however, there was a revival of interest in economic factors in evolution. Lewis Morgan was the American ethnologist who took the

[18] *Bracton and Azo*, Selden Society, vol. VIII (London, 1894), xiv.
[19] P. Vinogradoff, *Outlines of Historical Jurisprudence* (2 vols., London, 1920–2), 1.140.

THE AFTERMATH OF *ANCIENT LAW* 111

matriarchy view against Maine's patriarchy. He drew his data from similar sources to those of Adam Smith, the North American Indians and the ancient Greeks and Romans. In *Ancient Society* (1877) he developed a theory of social institutions, such as government, family and property, in which he emphasised the mode of subsistence and levels of technological advance as factors determining the development of social institutions. Morgan's work had great influence on Marx and Engels, who preferred his explanations to Maine's. Marx's annotations to Maine's *Lectures on the Early History of Institutions* have been published and vividly show his irritation with Maine's patrician air of authority. He calls him 'great Maine', 'der würdige Maine', comfortable Maine', and 'Maine als blockheaded Englishman', and notes that he is 'always mild when dealing with clergy and lawyers and higher class people generally'.[20]

When Engels spoke on Marx's grave in Highgate in 1883, he compared Marx with Darwin and claimed that he had discovered 'the elementary fact, hitherto concealed under a veil of ideological nonsense, that men, before they busy themselves with politics, science, art, religion, etc., must first eat, drink, clothe and house themselves; and therefore that the production of the means of life, and so the degree of economic development, constitute the foundation for all the institutions of the state – legal ideas, art, even religious ideas – and not the other way round'.[21]

Marx and his followers restored to thinking about legal change the emphasis on means of production, which Smith had introduced. As was brought out in a correspondence in *The Times*[22] in 1977, which was provoked by some remarks by Mrs Margaret Thatcher, it is to Adam Smith that we owe the idea that the prevailing modes of production largely determine the nature of social institutions, the form and extent of property rights and the nature of the relationships between men in society and their equality and inequality.

[20] L. Krader, *The Ethnological Notebooks of Karl Marx* (Assen, 1972), 289, 292, 299, 323 and 326.
[21] Cited by W. O. Chadwick, *The Secularization of the European Mind in the Nineteenth Century* (Cambridge, 1975), 60, from Marx–Engels, *Werke* (Berlin, 1962), 19.335,
[22] Begun by Lord Kaldor, 21 July 1977.

Smith's analysis was more subtle than that of Marx, since he allowed some weight to psychological factors in determining whether and how far the law of a society changed. Also he tended to avoid speculation about what kind of society would succeed that of the traders and manufacturers in the age of commerce. Marx and Engels, on the other hand, effectively excluded all other factors but economic conditions as determinants of legal change and they were very much concerned with the future after the fall of capitalism. Since they saw law as the expression of the will of those who control the means of production and in consequence wield political power, they came to the conclusion that in the truly communist state, there would be no need for law. It would just wither away. Until that day, however, law changes as economic life changes.[23]

Since they conceived of history as an evolutionary sequence through which all societies necessarily pass, and a society's law at each stage as necessarily determined by the prevailing economic conditions, Marx and Engels and their immediate followers may be regarded as among the last upholders of legal evolution in the strict sense. The problem now was, could one believe in legal evolution if one was not a Marxist?

A fourth group of objectors to legal evolution concentrated on the political consequences of looking at legal change in an evolutionary way. Maine's own attitude to the issues of his day was odd. He declared his opposition to democracy and popular government, on the ground that it was unprogressive. The innate conservatism of the ordinary man would make him oppose changes which science and knowledge showed the more enlightened members of society to be desirable. Yet in his later work, as Robson has pointed out, he 'displayed a sort of resentment that the world, which he had persistently announced as inherently opposed to change, was nevertheless changing continuously and rapidly before his eyes'.[24]

Whatever Maine's own politics may have been, his theories were used by others to justify opposition to proposals for legal reform generally. The lesson of legal evolution, it was said by his followers,

[23] For a good account of Marx's evolutionary ideas, L. J. Pospisil, *Anthropology of Law: a comparative theory* (New York, 1971), 151–65.   [24] 'Maine today', 176.

was that, whether we like it or not, the law somehow adapts itself gradually to new social and economic conditions. The fact that the common law, unlike continental law, remained uncodified reinforced whatever plausibility this view had. If the laws are written in the authoritative text of a code, they can only be changed either by amending the code, or by interpreting the words of the code in a new way, using, say, the technique of the fiction. But where the law is based on precedents, it is never stated finally once and for all. The judges can review an earlier case and discover that it is authority for a wider or a narrower proposition than earlier judges had thought. For they are bound by the decision, but not by the reasons given by the earlier judges for the decision; and the decision can be seen either as very much confined to its own facts or of much wider import than they thought. Given this system, it was possible to argue that the law is kept up to date from within its own resources. The training of English lawyers in the past has been essentially a training in cautiousness and conservatism, for it is based on what Roscoe Pound called 'the application of the judicial experience of the past to the judicial questions of the present'.[25] Legal evolution with its vague air of determinism was a great comfort to those who sought continuity in the law. The result was legal fatalism.

There was, however, a more sinister consequence of Maine's views which he cannot fairly be accused of intending. He observed that the secret of progressive societies was that they had set themselves definite goals:

It is impossible to overrate the importance to a nation or profession of having a distinct object to aim at in the pursuit of improvement. The secret of Bentham's immense influence in England during the past thirty years is his success in placing such an object before the country. He gave us a clear rule of reform. English lawyers of the last century were probably too acute to be blinded by the paradoxical commonplace that English law was the perfection of human reason, but they acted as if they believed it for want of any other principle to proceed upon. Bentham made the good of the community take precedence of every other object, and thus gave escape to a current which had long been trying to find its way outwards (ch. IV. p. 46).

Maine's followers found an alternative goal to Bentham's in his own generalisation that the movement of progressive societies had

[25] *The Spirit of the Common Law* (Boston, Mass., 1921), 182.

been from status to contract. The proposition was supported by the development of Roman law, but it was assumed to be equally applicable to the common law. It was seen as an expression of the working out of the idea of individual self-determination, of what Savigny called the 'will-theory'. This was the idea that the aim of law is to arrange for the fullest implementation of the individual's will, through contracts, through testaments, through the fullest disposition of one's property, and so on. Although Maine himself had cautiously said the movement had *hitherto* been from status to contract, his followers took it to be a general law of legal development; and evolution meant progress according to such general laws. Contract was more progressive than status, and so any legal rule which appeared to recreate status was condemned as retrograde. It was assumed that legal progress meant movement in the direction of greater self-determination for the individual, and that meant that no-one should be liable in law unless they had personally undertaken liability in a voluntary agreement or had personally been guilty of fault.

The will theory had a similar sort of absolute character for nineteenth-century lawyers to that which the doctrine of *laissez faire* had for nineteenth-century economists. For a while, the courts applied it to strike down anything which could be regarded as a restriction on freedom of contract, for example a covenant by which one party undertook not to compete with the other party after leaving his employment. On the other hand, standard form contracts made with public corporations or large companies were enforced to the letter, however onerous they might be, since they were treated as the product of voluntary agreement. The fact that the party bound had no choice but to accept the terms offered, if he wanted the service, or if he wanted a job, was ignored. Differences of bargaining power were irrelevant.

The legislation putting married women in the same position as their husbands with regard to owning property of their own was hailed as a triumph of progress, although it ignored the fact that most wives, because of their household duties, had no opportunity of acquiring property, and English law gave the wife no rights to her husband's property.

It was not until the First World War that this movement lost its force in America. In the U.S.A. social legislation was declared unconstitutional on the same grounds. Workmen's compensation statutes imposing liability on employers without proof of fault, truck acts which prohibited contracts under which employees agreed to accept part of their wages in orders for goods in company shops rather than in cash, all were struck down as being opposed to the great law of evolution from status to contract.[26]

The opposition to this individualist trend was stronger in Britain than in the U.S.A., and was traced by A. V. Dicey in his *Law and Public Opinion in England during the nineteenth century*,[27] published in 1905. He called it collectivism and argued that it was the product of several factors: the factory movement, the development of trade unionism after the defeat of Chartism in 1848, the modification of economic theories in the direction of socialism, the change in the commercial system from management by private persons to control by corporate bodies, and the introduction of household suffrage. Their cumulative effect on the law could be observed in the extension of the idea of protection of those in need, the restriction of freedom of contract (for example in favour of tenant farmers), the recognition of combinations of workers, and the equalisation of advantages through compulsory elementary education and the passing of employers' liability and workmen's compensation statutes. Dicey concluded that such legislation was deviating farther and farther from the lines laid down by Bentham, since public opinion 'is guided far less by the force of argument than by the stress of circumstances', and so 'the logic of events leads... to the extension and the development of legislation which bears the impress of collectivism' (pp. 301–2). The more collectivism advanced, the more it seemed to disprove the validity of the movement from status to contract.

VINOGRADOFF

The most prominent jurist to write in English in the tradition of Maine attempted to reconcile his theories with the objections raised against them. This was Sir Paul Vinogradoff (1854–1925), a Russian who in 1904 became Professor of Jurisprudence at Oxford, thus occupying the Chair held by Maine himself on his return from

[26] R. Pound, *Interpretations of Legal History* (Cambridge, 1923; reprinted Cambridge, Mass., 1946), 53–68.   [27] 2nd edn (London, 1914), 219ff; 260ff.

India. Vinogradoff was educated in Moscow, where there was a tradition of relating legal studies to social and economic history.

Curiously this tradition is linked with Adam Smith, through Smith's pupil, S. E. Desnitsky, a Ukrainian, who was sent by the Russian government, together with a colleague, I. A. Tretyakov, to study under Smith and John Millar in Glasgow. They remained there for six years, although Desnitsky's stay was nearly cut short after he pulled off the wig of the professor who was choir master, and was arraigned before a university tribunal for the offence. On their return to Russia, both Desnitsky and Tretyakov were appointed to Chairs of Law at Moscow University. Their works have recently been analysed by Mr A. H. Brown,[28] who has shown that their ideas were clearly derivative of Smith and Millar. Desnitsky especially championed the comparative historical method and the stadial theory of development, Furthermore, they upheld those ideas against a good deal of opposition. Desnitsky has been described by Russian legal historians as 'the Father of Russian Jurisprudence', and it is not unreasonable to think that enough of his ideas on the relations of law and the social and economic development of society survived to influence the young Vinogradoff at Moscow University a century later.[29]

In his unfinished *Outlines of Historical Jurisprudence*, published in 1920–2, Vinogradoff accepted Maitland's general criticism of Maine, but believed that Maine's comparative historical method was still valid, provided that inferences were 'preceded by a careful study of individual cases'. The aim would be to show the 'formation, development and decay' of particular legal institutions (1.149). Despite this apparently more cautious approach to comparative jurisprudence, Vinogradoff could not resist the temptation to arrange the material of legal history 'in accordance with the

---

[28] 'S. E. Desnitsky, Adam Smith and the Nakaz of Catherine II', *Oxford Slavonic Papers*, 7 (1974), 42–59; 'Adam Smith's First Russian Followers', *Essays on Adam Smith*, ed. A. S. Skinner and T. Wilson (Oxford, 1975), 247–73; 'The Father of Russian Jurisprudence: the Legal Thought of S. E. Desnitskii', *Russian Law: Historical and Political Perspectives*, ed. W. E. Butler (Leyden, 1977), 117–40.

[29] Another Russian admirer of Maine, contemporary with Vinogradoff, was M. Kovalevsky (1851–1916) whose main work, showing Maine's influence, was translated into French as *Coutume contemporaine et loi ancienne* (Paris, 1893). See *Encyclopedia of Social Sciences*, VIII (1933), 595.

divisions and relations of ideas rather than with dates' (I.155). This ideological approach to historical jurisprudence produced six stages of legal evolution.

First, there is the stage of totemistic society, in which 'there is not much technical law' (I.158). This stage is best left by the lawyers to the anthropologists. The second stage is tribal law, the account of which is in fact based on early Indo-European societies. In particular, Vinogradoff sees the tribal legal authority at this stage as declaring the law rather than making it. 'The ancient law-giver never considers himself as issuing an order to particular persons, or the community in general: his primary function is to *find the law* and give expression to the sense of the community in regard to juridical acts' (I.361). This idea, that law in tribal societies is 'declared', is an important feature of both early Roman and early Germanic law and was forcefully stated by Maine (*Ancient Law*, ch. II, pp. 18–20).

The third stage of Vinogradoff's scheme is civic law, defined by its relation to city life. Its rules 'depend on one dominant fact – the nature of the city commonwealth' (II.2). The sanctions for legal rules are now imposed in the name of the government of a political state. The main example of this stage is Greek law, and Vinogradoff seized the opportunity to discuss a system of law which had not aroused the attention of scholars to anything like the degree which Roman law had done. It is difficult to separate the Roman law of this stage of development from that of the later period when Rome had grown from a city state into an Empire. Greek law, on the other hand, remained at the stage of civic law.

Up to this point the criterion which characterised each stage of law was the type of society. Law changed as society and its form of government changed. For the remaining three stages, however, Vinogradoff altered his criterion to the kind of legal ideas which the society produced. He could only sketch their main features.

The fourth stage, that of medieval law, is blatantly relevant only to Europe. It consists of a combination of two systems of law, which Vinogradoff admits appeared to a great extent antagonistic to each other: feudal law and canon law. The first derived its validity from divine guidance, and applied to all men; the second, based on the economy of the manor, referred to the ties of fidelity. Yet, says

Vinogradoff with ingenuity, 'it is not a mere accident that the two laws – the feudal and the Canon – are found growing on the same soil. Their dualism is the necessary consequence of their extreme onesidedness. Feudal law has too narrow and Canon too wide a basis...even technically the one cannot exist without being supplemented by the other' (1.159).

The fifth stage is individualistic jurisprudence, which gradually superseded medieval law. This stage is said to be characterised by the tendency of the legal mind to base its concepts on individualism; legal thinkers considered social relations from the point of view of the individual and aimed to assure the individual maximum happiness and minimum pain. The tendency reached its culmination in the mid-nineteenth century.

The sixth stage is socialistic jurisprudence, of which Dicey had traced the beginnings. This phase is marked by less emphasis on the individual and more attention to social forces. Vinogradoff rejected the materialistic fatalism of Marxism but looked forward to the implementation of an idealistic socialism in the (distant) future.

Vinogradoff's scheme reveals the difficulties of postulating a credible series of stages of legal evolution.[30] In the first place, it tries to harmonise two different evolutionary principles, one that legal change is determined by different social conditions and the other that it is the product of the gradual unfolding of certain ideas; but he was unable to show their relationship with each other. He himself recognised the problem. In the earliest stages, those of totemistic and tribal law, legal change is wholly determined by social and economic conditions; in the later stages, individualistic and socialistic, it is the result of the pressure of ideas. 'Ideas', he said, 'do not entirely get their own way in real life; they are embodied in facts, and these latter appear influenced largely by material necessities and forces. It is not without importance for the development of legal principles whether the atmosphere surrounding them is that of a pastoral, an agricultural, or an industrial community' (1.159). But he could not explain the mechanism of interaction of facts and ideas in the promotion of legal change.

Secondly, Vinogradoff's scheme, in its earliest stages, has a

[30] J. Stone, *Social Dimensions of Law and Justice* (London, 1966), 142–3.

universal character, being based on 'materials... from all inhabited parts of the world', yet it becomes, in the later stages, 'restricted in the main to the evolution of juridical ideas within the circle of European civilization' (1.158). As he admitted, it had no place for 'important variations, such as the juridical systems of Brahmanism, of Islam, of the Talmud' (1.158).

Having acknowledged these difficulties, Vinogradoff suddenly seems to realise that the best way out of the dilemma is to abandon the attempt to arrange the stages in any sort of order. 'The essential point is to recognize the value of *historical types* as the foundation of a theory of law.' (1.160). Other scholars were reaching this conclusion at about the same time, in England in a pragmatic way and in Germany in a more theoretical way.

In England, the recognition of historical types was based on a re-appraisal of method. Whereas previously legal evolutionists had regarded their method as at the same time historical *and* comparative, now a clear distinction was made between the two approaches. James Bryce, who later became Lord Bryce, had been Regius Professor of Civil Law in Oxford, and as such had to face the need to demonstrate the relevance of Roman legal methods for prospective English lawyers. He divided the methods of legal science into four: metaphysical (or *a priori*), analytic, historical and comparative.

The first advantage of the historical method, in his view, is that it reveals not similarities but differences. It explains doctrines and rules as arising 'from special conditions in the country or people where the law in question arose. All law is a compromise between the past and the present, between tradition and convenience... It conceives of national character and the circumstances of national growth as creative forces' (Bryce had studied in Germany). Secondly, the historical method indicates that the rules which prevail at any given time are the product of that time, 'and must undergo the same change and decay which previous rules have experienced'. It must avoid lapsing into 'mere antiquarianism on the one side, or into general political and social history on the other'.[31]

The weak point of the historical method is 'that it is more

[31] *Studies in History and Jurisprudence* (2 vols., New York, 1901), II.617–18.

applicable to the law of any particular country than to the theory of law in general'. It must, therefore, be supplemented by the comparative method, which collects rules and institutions found in every developed legal system, or most of them, notes their similarities and differences and 'seeks thereby to construct a system which shall be Natural because it embodies what men otherwise unlike have agreed in feeling to be essential, Philosophical because it gets below words and names and discovers identity of substance under diversity of description, and Serviceable, because it shows by what particular means the ends which all (or most) systems pursue have been best attained' (II.619). By studying the differences in combination with the historical method we can 'disengage what is local or accidental or transient in legal doctrine from what is general, essential and permanent' (II.620). In other words, the two methods together will show what institutions, doctrines and trends frequently recur in developed systems of law. Bryce admits that this approach is best suited to advanced legal systems, and particularly, in view of the availability of materials, to a comparison of the methods and doctrines of Roman and English law.

Although some of Bryce's essays in this field, such as his comparison of the Roman Empire and the British Empire in India, now appear rather dated, he made many perceptive observations at a more technical level. But the historical–comparative method had moved a long way from legal evolution as it was understood forty years before.

The parallel movement in Germany begins with the publication of Ferdinand Tönnies' seminal work, *Gemeinschaft und Gesellschaft*,[32] in 1887. Tönnies developed his argument from Maine's treatment of the movement of progressive societies from status to contract, and portrayed the 'tragic conflict' that resulted from the emergence of two contrasting types of social grouping. The first, *Gemeinschaft*, is a community or fellowship of those sharing, to some degree, a common way of life, such as a family, college or trade guild. The second, *Gesellschaft*, is a limited relationship based on the 'rational will', the desire of the parties to achieve some particular purpose, usually by contract. These are 'ideal' types in the sense that they are not to be found in a pure

[32] Ed. C. P. Loomis as *Community and Society* (1957), Harper Torchbook edn, 1963.

form in any actual societies, but they provide a tool for characterising particular social relationships.

Although Tönnies noted the relevance of his two basic types to law, in that law is clearly more suited to deal with the second than the first, he was more interested in the social implications of the distinction. However, his younger contemporary, Max Weber, in his *Wirtschaft und Gesellschaft* (1922), not only formulated a set of ideal types of rigorously defined social situations, but also applied them to legal development (ch. VII, 'Sociology of Law'). As his editor, Max Rheinstein, explains, Weber asked

> what would be the characteristics of a society in which all the precepts for social conduct are obeyed because they have always been obeyed and have thus become accepted as inveterate, or because the ruler is regarded as 'charismatically' qualified to be the man of destiny; or because its governmental system is carried on in accordance with a set of rules which have been worked out rationally and are regarded as the 'right' ones? Situations of such 'pure' type have never existed in history. They are artificial constructs similar to the pure constructs of geometry.[33]

Yet they were based on deep historical research;[34] one of Weber's earliest works was a study of the relationship between the development of Roman agriculture and Roman public and private law. He used the same sources as the legal evolutionists to construct models or types, which could then be used to characterise the particular social or legal relationship, irrespective of the society in which it occurred. Weber's 'ideal types' imply no evaluation and they are divorced from the historical process. They are intended to facilitate the study and comparison of actual systems, irrespective of time and place.

[33] Introduction to *Max Weber on Law and Society* (New York, 1967), xxix.
[34] For Weber's attitude to historical data, see D. G. MacRae, *Weber*, Fontana Modern Masters series (London, 1974), 45–6, 64–5.

Conclusion

I have used the term legal evolution to describe a group of theories which claim to explain legal change not merely in historical terms but as proceeding according to certain determinate stages, or in a certain pre-determined manner. In their fully developed form, such theories were essentially a nineteenth-century phenomenon and did not long survive the end of the century. They were produced by thinkers who were, on the whole, satisfied with the state of the law as it was, and although they would have liked to see certain technical reforms, they were apprehensive about the threat of wholesale and dramatic change in the law. Savigny was concerned to resist the scrapping of the traditional Roman law, as it had been adapted to German conditions, in favour of a new codification. Maine's attitude to Bentham and Austin was sometimes equivocal, but he was certainly unsympathetic to radical reform and very suspicious of the view that English law was whatever the sovereign legislature resolved to make it. The idea of legal evolution appealed to conservative legal thinkers, especially perhaps to academic conservatives who liked to think of themselves as progressive.

Legal evolution was also closely linked with the position of Roman law. In Germany, the earlier historical school under Hugo had shown that what passed for Roman law was a rationalised version, produced by the natural lawyers, which obscured the way in which its institutions had come to be what they were, so that their true meaning could not be understood. Niebuhr's discovery in 1816 of the Verona palimpsest of Gaius' *Institutes*, the main source for classical Roman law before Justinian's *Corpus Juris*, dramatised the unique status of Roman law, so far as the records of its development were concerned. It was documented by written sources, from its earliest beginnings as the law of a tribal society clustered on the banks of the Tiber in the sixth century B.C. to its peak as the law of a world empire in the second century A.D., and thereafter as the law of a declining society. Savigny converted the stages of this development into a general law of evolution, applicable to certain types of society of which he approved.

In England, Maine inherited a traditional view of long standing that associated general legal theory with Roman law. English law has always been strong on its legal rules but weak on its legal theory. Whereas English law has remained relatively free of Roman influences, English jurisprudence has traditionally turned for inspiration to the current continental theories, necessarily based on Roman law.[1] So Austin naturalised many Pandectist ideas and passed them off as universal legal concepts. Maine was less dependent on Savigny than was Austin on the Pandectists, but he seems to have felt instinctively that the stages in the development of Roman law were generally applicable to progressive societies, and that in turn confirmed his view that Roman law was a necessary ingredient in the courses on general jurisprudence, the scientific aspects of law, which were demanded by the Committee on Legal Education. If the new courses were to have a theoretical basis, the only practical alternative to the systematic analytical approach was an historical theory, and such a theory necessarily involved Roman law. In an age when classical literature was regarded as a necessary component in the education of a civilised man, it seemed quite natural that Roman law should form part of the preparation of an educated lawyer, not for its technical details, but for what it could teach him about the nature of law itself.

Adam Smith's theory of legal development, although older than Savigny's or Maine's, seems to us more modern. It was based on the study of a larger number of societies than either of theirs; it used Roman law considerably, but did not give it that special pre-eminent position which it enjoyed in the nineteenth-century theories. Furthermore, Smith is less dogmatic. He attributes the main influence, among factors affecting legal change to the mode of subsistence, but he also recognises national character and

[1] P. Stein, *Roman Law and English Jurisprudence yesterday and today* (inaugural lecture) (Cambridge, 1969).

tradition, and generally gives a good deal of weight to psychological factors, in determining the details of legal rules. The notion of the impartial spectator approving the level of punishment, or deciding what agreements should be enforced as contracts, according to the views prevailing at the time in his society, is especially congenial to modern ideas.

The present climate of opinion is not favourable to evolutionary ideas in the social studies. In the first place, the notion of evolution tends to be associated with the idea of the progress of society. The late eighteenth and mid-nineteenth centuries were ages of optimism; there was a general underlying feeling that, despite occasional set-backs, society was getting better all the time. Since 1914 we have lost this confidence that the future will be better than the past. Despite enormous technological advances and improvements in general living-standards, we are no longer sure that, in social relationships, we are necessarily progressing. Social change is accompanied by legal change, but it is not part of an inexorable ascent to Utopia.

Secondly, we have abandoned the idea that the methods of classical physics can be applied to the study of social phenomena. The certainties of the natural sciences themselves have been shown to be less secure than was believed. As A. Giddens put it, there has been 'an erosion, in the twentieth century, of faith in scientific knowledge as the exemplar of all knowledge and of the ranking of human cultures according to how far they have progressed towards the attainment of scientific rationalism'.[2] So the image of science, which gave legal evolution so much attraction, has been tarnished.

This distrust of the methods of traditional science has been accompanied by a rejection of general schemes designed to provide explanations of institutional change on a universal basis. We now concentrate more on the unique character of particular societies, on the factors which made certain societies change in one way and others in different ways. In view of the complexity of different cultures, it hardly seems feasible to try to explain the origin and development of the basic institutions of any private law system, independently of the social circumstances peculiar to particular societies.

[2] *New Rules of Sociological Method* (London, 1976), 130.

Even if it were feasible, it seems less worth while today than it did in Adam Smith's day or Maine's day. This is because our view of the function of law in society has changed. When Maine wrote, the prevailing opinion on the function of law was not very different from what it had been in Adam Smith's day. There was a basic distinction between public and private law. Public law was concerned with the interests of the community as a whole, and was confined to the preservation of the integrity of the state from external attack and the preservation of order within. Apart from that limited function, it was felt, people should be allowed to get on with their lives as they thought best for themselves, without interference from anyone else. There had to be legal provision for special categories, such as the insane, or the poor (and the poor law was an important instrument of social policy), but for most people public law hardly impinged on their lives at all. Private law was concerned with disputes over property rights and was designed to give the owner of property the maximum possible enjoyment and freedom of disposition.

Today all this is changed. The distinction between public and private law has largely disappeared. Every private law dispute seems to have a public dimension to it. The sale of a house involves planning considerations, and the possibility of public works, such as a new road, in the back garden. A divorce has a social security aspect; a road accident has a social insurance aspect. Over every legal relationship, brooding ominously, hangs the spectre of taxation. The fact is that most of the disputes that arise today involve administrative law in one form or another, and administrative law is primarily concerned with the application of general standards of reasonableness and fairness, which involves the exercise of discretion according to the values and ideas of today.[3]

For Maine, as for Adam Smith, the law was still concerned with deciding rights and duties; the legal process was a matter of black or white. A debt was owed or it was not owed, a thing was possessed or it was not. Either full compensation for injury was due or nothing at all. Nowadays, the law is much more a matter of compromise, of adjustment of competing claims. Consequently, we envisage the law as a process of balancing interests, of preferring

[3] R. M. Unger, *Law in Modern Society* (New York, 1976), 192–237.

one social value to another as the prevailing consensus in the view of the judges seems to dictate. They no longer purport to apply legal rules in a formal way, without regard for the consequences; they consciously try to adjust their application to the social purposes which the rules were designed to fulfil.

In view of these changes, the identification of patterns of development in the basic private law institutions, contract, property, succession and so on, does not seem to be so relevant to contemporary issues today as it did in the eighteenth and nineteenth centuries. The recognition of such patterns is still of great historical interest, and is essential for a proper appreciation of the traditional functions of private law concepts; but it no longer has the actuality which it had even a hundred years ago.

Does this mean that the ideas of the legal evolutionists were all in vain, merely a curious episode in the history of legal thought? By no means, for the movement had some permanent results in the way we look at law today. In the first place, many of the detailed ideas of the evolutionists have passed into our ways of thought, not as generally applicable laws of evolution but as models or types of legal reasoning or of legal development.[4] We know that they are never found in their pure form in any actual system of law, but they enable us to characterise aspects of legal systems in a way that expresses their persistent elements more vividly than a detailed catalogue. Where empirical reality is too complex, a model enables us to see the wood for the trees. We can then identify underlying similarities and differences and can test hypotheses by more detailed study. These models or types are now part of the grammar of general jurisprudence.

In a more general way, we take for granted the value and importance of studying legal institutions comparatively, and of tracing modern legal doctrines back to the social circumstances in which they were first introduced. When we note differences in the laws of the two countries, we instinctively look for differences in their respective social orders; we assume that there is a correlation between the two. We no longer try to arrange the differences according to stages or patterns of development. We realise that the socio-legal development even of a particular society is a complex

---

[4] A recent example in M. B. Hooker, *Legal Pluralism* (Oxford, 1975), 67, 146, 444.

CONCLUSION

matter, which cannot be reduced to a neat formula. But the point is that we take it for granted that any adequate exposition of legal institutions and legal doctrines must take into account the social context in which they have grown up. We think it absurd to try to describe legal change in isolation from social and economic changes. And yet that is precisely what legal thinkers were doing before the legal evolutionists captured the public imagination. Without the pioneering work of the historical jurisprudence, contemporary sociological jurisprudence would not have the general acceptance which it enjoys. It is perhaps strange that sociological methods should have been applied to the laws of past societies, or of contemporary primitive societies, before being applied to our own law, but doubtless, as has been suggested,[5] scholars are able to be more objective in their appraisal of other societies than they are of their own society.

[5] J. Stone, *Social Dimensions of Law and Justice* (London, 1966), 111.

Index

Abdy, J. T. 82
adoption 94, 107
Allen, C. K. 89n
American Indians 7, 17, 18, 21, 24, 25, 30, 34, 38, 75, 92, 111
Anglo-Saxon law 92, 107–9
anthropology 101–6
Arabs 21, 36
Austin, J. 71–2, 85, 97, 122, 123

Bachofen, J. J. 101
Bacon, F. 47n, 78
Barbeyrac, J. 3
Bentham, J. 68, 69, 70–2, 89, 94, 97, 113, 115, 122
Blackstone, W. 69, 70, 83
Bohannan, P. J. 105
Bopp, F. 91
Bordeaux 17
Bracton 109, 110
Brougham, H. 71
Brown, A. H. 116
Bryce, J. 119–20
Buckle, H. T. 100
Burke, E. 57–9, 74, 75
Burrow, J. 77, 85, 99

Campbell, T. D. 45
canon law 117–18
Carthage 37
Christians, early 8
Clark, E. C. 86
Clarke, S. 10
codes, ancient 93, 103
codification 52, 59, 71–2, 74
Coleridge, S. T. 64
common law 69–70, 113
Comte, A. 74, 76–8, 83, 89
Connington, J. 78
conservatism, of legal evolutionists 112–15

contract, law of 11, 13, 28, 39–40, 98, 105, 114–15; *see also* 'status to contract'
Cooper, C. P. 72n
crime, law of 26, 28, 42, 105
cyclical patterns in history 17, 31–2, 60–2

Dalrymple, J. 23–9
Darwin, C. 88n, 100, 111
Desnitsky, S. E. 116
Dicey, A. V. 115, 118

Education, Committee on Legal 78–9, 85, 123
Egyptians, ancient 20, 26
Eldon, Lord 95
Empson, W. 74, 75
Engels, F. 111–12
equity 74, 82, 84, 94–5
Essenes 8

Family 6–7, 34, 43, 49, 84, 95–6, 102, 106, 108–9
Feaver, G. 88n
feudal law 23, 27, 38, 117–18
fictions, legal 81–2, 94, 98
Forbes, D. 8n, 26
formalism, legal 104
four-stage theory 19, 23–5, 28–9, 33–6
Frederick the Great 52
Friedmann, W. 65

Gaius, *Institutes* of 122
Genesis 6–7, 24, 35
German law 61–3
Gibbon, E. 54–6
Giddens, A. 124
Gierke, O. von 110
Gluckman, M. 105–6
Goguet, A.-Y. 19–23, 26, 27
Goths 32

129

INDEX

Göttingen 53, 54, 72, 73
Gracchi 32
Greeks, ancient 17–18, 20, 30, 36, 58, 78, 117
Grote, G. 77–8, 83, 84, 85, 89, 90, 91, 98
Grotius, H. 3–8, 30, 39, 41, 51

Hardwicke, Lord 24
Harrington, J. 31, 32
Hayward, A. 60n, 64, 69, 74
Hebrews 20; *see also* Genesis
Hegel, G. W. F. 101
Heineccius, J. G. 7, 53, 55
Herder, J. G. 57–9
Hindu law 92–4, 106
History, legal 106–10
Hobbes, T. 1, 2, 11, 31, 51
Hoebel, E. A. 104
Home, H., *see* Kames, Lord
Homer, 18, 35, 39
Hugo, G. 54–6, 57, 59, 64, 69
Hume, D. 12–14, 15, 23, 26, 27, 29, 30, 45, 54, 91
Hutcheson, F. 9–12, 14, 27, 30, 33

Iroquois 17–18, 58

Jefferson, T. 79
Jeffrey, F. 49, 50
Jhering, R. von 65–8, 89n
Jones, Sir W. 92
justice, and property 13–14, 33

Kames, Lord 23–9, 30, 43, 46
Kemble, J. M. 92, 107
Kovalevsky, M. 116n

Lafitau, J.-F. 17–18, 20, 30, 58
Leechman, W. 9
Lewes, G. H. 85
liberty, natural 11, 45–6
Locke, J. 1–3, 38
Long, G. 79–82, 86, 98
love stories 44
Lyell, C. 88

Machiavelli, N. 31
McLennan, J. F. 83–6, 102
Maine, H. S. x, 71, 82, 85, 86–98, 99–115, 116, 122, 123, 125
Maitland, F. W. 63, 106, 108–10, 116
marriage 16, 41–4, 49, 102
Marx, K. 111–12
matriarchy 49, 102

Meek, R. L. 19
Merivale, C. 99
Middle Temple, Committee on Legal Education at 79–80
Mill, James 83
Mill, John Stuart 77, 78, 83, 85
Millar, J. 23, 30, 46–50, 58, 72, 85, 102, 116
Momigliano, A. D. 18, 55
Montesquieu, Baron 15–20, 23, 24, 25, 26, 30, 31, 46, 54, 56, 57, 64, 74, 77, 83, 90
Morgan, L. H. 102, 110–11
Müller, M. 91

Napoleon 59
natural law 3–11, 14, 15, 51–2
nature, state of 1, 11, 12
Nicolaos of Damascus 39
Niebuhr, B. G. 90–1, 122

Pandectists 71, 72, 123
Park, J. J. 72, 73
Patriarchs, Biblical 22, 25, 35
patriarchy 96, 102, 106–8
philology, comparative 91–2
Pollock, F. x, 89n, 98, 106
positive law 4, 10, 16, 72, 89–90
positivism 76–7, 89
Pound, R. 113
Proculians and Sabinians 56
property
  community of 8, 107–9
  law of 13, 15, 25, 27, 30, 32–41, 105
  origin of 5–7
Pufendorf, S. 3–8, 13, 30, 39, 41, 51
Pütter, J. S. 53

Reddie, James 75–6
Reddie, John 73–4
religion and early law 103
Rheinstein, M. 121
rights
  classification of 33–4
  perfect and imperfect 10, 33
Rivière, P. 83n
Robson, W. A. 102, 112
Roman law 15, 41–3, 48, 53–6, 61–3, 65–8, 71, 80–2, 86–7, 91, 92, 94–7, 99, 106, 107, 114, 117, 121–2
Rome, ancient 32, 37–8, 90
Rousseau, J. J. 58

Savigny, F. K. von 56–65, 66, 67, 69, 71, 72–8, 80, 81, 82, 83, 89, 90, 91, 97, 101, 110, 114, 122, 123

INDEX

Severus, Alexander 95
Smith, Adam 23, 29–46, 53, 54, 58, 74, 83, 110, 111–12, 116, 123, 125
Smith, Sir Thomas 47n
social contract 1–3, 11, 12
society, progress of 47–8, 77, 90; *see also* four-stage theory
sociology 77
Stair, Lord 24
statistics 47, 100
'status to contract' theory 84–5, 96–7, 114–15
Stewart, D. 9n, 30n
succession on death 41–2, 98, 105

Tacitus 35
Tartars 21, 35, 36
Thatcher, M. 111

themistes 84, 93
Thibaut, A. F. J. 62, 64, 71
Thomasius, C. 51–2
Tönnies, F. 120–1
Tretyakov, I. A. 116
Turgot, A. R. J. 19
types, historical 119–21
Tytler, F. (Lord Woodhouselee) 49

village communities 107–9
Vinogradoff, P. 115–21

Wales, laws of 92
Weber, M. 121
Wolff, C. 51–2
Wood, T. ix

Yorke, C. 24